PRAISE FOR *THE VIRTUAL LEADER*

"While the pandemic is still redefining what modern working space looks like, this is the time to care for—and trust—the digital employee experience. At Microsoft, we've built technologies to enable all 175,000 employees across 74 countries to remotely develop cutting-edge software and services every day. In this book, Takako shares her best practices for how to be a successful virtual leader. From the workplace setup to meeting logistics to mental health, Takako gives you a total package to excel in this new world."

—Alex Chiang, Principal Software Engineering Manager, Microsoft

"*The Virtual Leader* is mandatory reading for any remote leader seeking to evolve their leadership style. Based on real-world experience and proven methods, the book is full of practical and actionable advice and strategies for remote leadership."

—Michael Vermillion, Senior Managing Director,
Global Business Intelligence, J.D. Power

"This book is a must-read for you to stay on top of the current remote work trend that's dramatically changing the way people collaborate. Get in-depth insights from an experienced facilitator of 24/7 engagements with colleagues dispersed across time zones, countries, and continents. *The Virtual Leader* provides hope and a guidebook on how to thrive in the midst of the most significant work development of our time."

—Diane Chen, former Senior Global Brand Design Manager,
Procter & Gamble, and former Creative Director,
Worldwide Brand Experience, Lenovo

"Building a great remote culture is critical to the success of all remote teams. Takako's insights in this space and her overall expertise in managing remote teams are beneficial to all managers making the transition."

—Andy Tryba, CEO, Gigster

"*The Virtual Leader* serves as a 'best practices' reference for navigating the virtual hybrid environment in our professional, personal, academic, and social lives. As a Harvard HealthTech Fellow, I regularly refer to Takako's work to structure how I engage with stakeholders across institutions, expertises, time zones, and industries, as we collaborate to develop novel medical technology. Takako's personal anecdotes give the reader unique insights and lessons learned, as she has developed a framework and a leadership style that can successfully motivate and empower virtual and decentralized teams."

—Nicky Agahari, HealthTech Fellow, Harvard Medical School

"As remote work is progressing rapidly due to the influences of COVID-19 and globalization, many companies are having a hard time managing employees and projects. Takako, the author of *The Virtual Leader*, has managed remote work from an early stage across national borders. The experience and knowledge she gained led her to develop the virtual workplace techniques she covers in the book, which will be of great value to managers everywhere."

—Akihiko Morisawa, President and CEO, The Morisawa Inc.

THE VIRTUAL LEADER

THE
VIRTUAL
LEADER

How to manage a remote workplace

TAKAKO HIRATA

Matt Holt Books
An Imprint of BenBella Books, Inc.
Dallas, TX

The Virtual Leader copyright © 2022 by Takako Hirata

Matt Holt Books is an imprint of BenBella Books, Inc.
10440 N. Central Expressway
Suite 800
Dallas, TX 75231
benbellabooks.com
Send feedback to feedback@benbellabooks.com

Matt Holt and *BenBella* are federally registered trademarks.

Printed in the United States of America
10 9 8 7 6 5 4 3 2 1

Library of Congress Control Number: 2021948613
ISBN 9781637741245 (trade cloth)
ISBN 9781637741252 (ebook)

Copyediting by Jennifer Brett Greenstein
Proofreading by James Fraleigh and Cape Cod Compositors, Inc.
Indexing by Amy Murphy
Text design and composition by Aaron Edmiston
Cover design by Virsitil Inc.
Cover art by zaie / Adobe Stock
Printed by Lake Book Manufacturing

To Aina.
My love, my life, my light

CONTENTS

Introduction: A New World   1

CHAPTER 1   The Three Places   9

CHAPTER 2   Trust in the Remote Workplace   27

CHAPTER 3   Forms of Communication in the Remote World   45

CHAPTER 4   Reinvesting Your Savings   59

CHAPTER 5   Mental Health in the Remote Workplace   73

CHAPTER 6   The Meeting   89

CHAPTER 7   On Minimizing Distractions   105

CHAPTER 8   The New Leader   123

CHAPTER 9   The New Employee   141

CHAPTER 10   Remote Working and the Changing Meaning of Leadership   159

Epilogue: Takeaways   169

Acknowledgments   179

Notes   183

Index   191

A NEW WORLD

Where were you when you first realized that the pandemic was going to change the world? I remember where I was with vivid clarity—in my apartment in Tokyo. I was packing my suitcase for another international trip, listening to my daughter chatter on her phone in the background. In a few hours, I was to board a flight to New York—thirteen hours direct—to attend a meeting with a major marketing company in the city. It was an important meeting. As Rohto's head of international business development, I was meeting with our United States division to come up with a plan to market our eye drops; they're a particularly popular product, and I was thinking of partnering with the New York Yankees for a campaign. A big campaign, to say the least.

Hours before I was to get into a taxi to head to Haneda Airport, I received a notification that my flight was canceled. This didn't come as too much of a surprise; flights were being canceled across the globe, governments were starting to mull over lockdowns, and we'd had our first confirmed case in Japan several weeks earlier. I shrugged it off and just figured that we'd postpone the meeting, and we did.

That was the prevailing attitude at the time: postponing. School was postponed; my daughter's birthday party was postponed; dinner with my friends was postponed, as were doctor's appointments, soccer games, annual general meetings, college, and even the whole Olympics. Despite all that has happened over the last two years or so, this attitude hasn't quite gone away. As the vaccines start to flow, people get inoculated, and the world fights back against the virus, it's easy to believe that everything that was once postponed will now happen, all at once. Or put more simply, that the world is going to go back to what was once "normal."

By now, you've probably recognized that this isn't the case. The world has changed so much in a matter of months, and it now has a kind of momentum, or inertia, that's keeping it on the new path it has adopted. Our notions of what is normal have changed: school has changed; social gatherings have changed; travel has changed; hygiene standards have changed—and the changes are all-encompassing.

Work too has changed—fundamentally so—and it doesn't seem to be returning to what it once was.

Don't just take *my* word for it, however. Here are some facts:

- A survey by Microsoft of thirty thousand workers found that over 70 percent of workers wanted flexible, remote work options, even after the pandemic ended.[1]

- According to the American asset management firm Mercer, 94 percent of the *employers* it surveyed believed that their companies were as or more productive when working remotely, when compared to working from an office.[2]

- Gallup, the analytics firm based in Washington, DC, found that the longer the pandemic went on, the higher the number of American workers who wanted to work remotely *even after* the country reopened.[3]

- A survey of 669 executives by PWC, the multinational professional services firm, found that as many as 78 percent of CEOs agreed that remote working was here to stay for the long term.[4]

A list of relevant statistics would be endless, and more information about the endurance of remote work is simply a Google search away or will be on the front pages of tomorrow's financial papers. In fact, as I write this introduction, I'm reading headlines about how even Apple employees are resigning because their company will not allow them to work fully remotely![5]

I don't mean to suggest, however, that the full-time-work-from-home-every-day kind of remote environment is here to stay for everyone. Certain jobs simply cannot be done without meeting in person, and a sizable number of employees and leaders still do believe that being face-to-face with others is an essential fact of their working lives. All the same, it's clear that some form of remote work is here to stay. Why is this the case?

Prior to the pandemic, remote working was a realm reserved for a few specific positions like IT workers or customer care executives.

It was a perk for high-achieving team members who could take time to work from Brazil or the Alps or a niche option for some smaller startups that wanted to be hip and buck normal trends. During the pandemic, however, employers and workers both realized that working remotely wasn't particularly difficult, did not require any drastic adaptations or new technology, and was open to far more positions and industries than was previously thought. Most importantly for employers, as discussed above, it did not affect productivity.

For the companies themselves, the sudden change has allowed them to function much leaner. They no longer need as much real estate—which in certain cases can even be leased out—and they require fewer employees to keep the company running. Office equipment and other overhead costs are also unnecessary, giving employers a chance to redirect these savings to other ends.

For the workers themselves, the advent of remote work across the world has birthed a new age of flexibility. No longer having to attend a physical office every day means more time for other activities. More time for children and family. More time for hobbies. And more time for enjoying the comfort of their own home—or a beach in Hawaii, if they so wish.

We're going to explore all these reasons at length in the chapters to come, but I wanted to give you a very succinct taste of why the world *might* be reluctant to go back to a time when physical offices were the norm. I also want to put a disclaimer here: all the advantages of remote work that I mentioned above are what you get if you can do remote work *right*. It's not easy to do, and requires initiative, boldness, and a lot of introspection. The purpose of my book is to teach you this: I want to help you learn how you can lead your office into this new, virtual world.

Going remote means more than just having your team members log on every day—from wherever they are—at 9 AM and log off at 5 PM. There are several new factors that you have to take into consideration as a leader when you're no longer working out of an office where you see your team in person every day.

Physical separation and a reliance on technology can lead to both miscommunication and feelings of isolation. Working from home can also mean having to deal with constant interruptions from children, pets, and delivery workers. Meetings can be hard to coordinate when your team lives across different continents and time zones. In addition, your own team will seek new forms of guidance from you and will expect a different kind of leadership from what you practiced back when you worked out of an office.

The barriers to successfully implementing a remote-working environment and the ways to overcome them aren't going to be discussed in a single paragraph: that's why I wrote a whole book about them. But why let *me* tell you about it all? What do I have to offer you?

I've been a remote leader long before the onset of the pandemic. As the head of international business development at Rohto for nearly four years, I oversee five subsidiary CEOs, dozens of direct reports, and more than a hundred employees across five continents. I'm based in Tokyo now, but have been living the Zoom/virtual/work-from-home (WFH) lifestyle for over half a decade. Over that time, I've built a repertoire of wisdom, techniques, and tricks that will be valuable to remote leaders anywhere in the world. My work has also taken me to the United States, the European Union, South Africa, Central America, Asia, and Australia, causing me to not only count how many passport pages I have left but also approach remote work and its adoption from a global perspective.

I wanted to write this book *now* because I've seen three generations suddenly thrust into a world of work that they neither foresaw nor were prepared for. This book is for the next generation of leaders, who will now be working remotely without ever knowing what it was like to work out of a consolidated office. It's also for an older generation of leaders, now pushed into a world where their previous values and leadership styles are no longer *as* important. And finally, it's also for that middle generation of leaders, who have some tangential relationship to both offices and virtual environments but don't know how to make the most of the latter.

This book is for leaders of startups that will never have an office or physical location and for older companies that will be transitioning from an office to a remote environment. The content is relevant for offices that are wholly remote, as well as those that choose to adopt some mix of a physical and virtual environment—also known in today's lingo as hybrid offices.

Part of the reason I wished to write this book was also to question the age-old strictures that bind work culture in Japan. Our notions of what work "really" consists of are far too rigid and are due to be reexamined from a new perspective. It is my hope that through addressing how remote working has changed the world, the knowledge in this book can also help my fellow Japanese colleagues rethink work culture as a whole.

The book is broadly divided into three parts.

Part one covers how to adapt to the new normal and the importance of conserving the notion of the "office," even while moving online. Chapter one covers the idea of rituals and how they give shape to our idea of work and the office. Chapter two covers trust and the necessity that it be carefully cultivated in virtual environments. Chapter three covers how communication has changed and grown as we move online and how we can best make use of technology to communicate clearly and efficiently.

Part two examines the virtual environment and how we can optimize it to the advantage of our team members and our own leadership. Chapter four considers how companies can make themselves leaner and use the money saved to reinvest in their teams. Chapter five consists of a detailed look at mental and physical health and how to best maintain both when working isolated from one another. Chapter six is devoted wholly to the dreaded meeting and best practices around them. Chapter seven considers the distractions that workers face when going remote and how to minimize them for maximum focus.

Part three focuses on the new aspects of leadership demanded by a remote-working world. Chapter eight is an examination of how our ideas of leadership change when moving to remote-only environments. Chapter nine considers the new expectations of employees, now that the world has mass-adopted remote work, and whether hybrid work may be the answer to our new conundrums. In chapter ten, I will go deeper into my personal experiences and dig for the wisdom I have learned in the last five years or so. Finally, the epilogue recaps key takeaways from each chapter.

Most chapters begin with a case study to illuminate a single issue related to remote working. I then outline the details of the problem, discuss the techniques to address it, and provide some of my own personal tips and tricks for remote leaders. The book also includes two short profiles/interviews of my remote-working associates who had experiences relevant to the chapter topics.

It is my hope that by the end of this book, you will not only be equipped to lead your office into this new world of work but also be well adapted for any more shocks or sudden changes to office culture that may arise in the future. Begin this book with an open mind, and be prepared to change some of your most cherished notions about leadership and work itself. It's very rare that the world changes its views on something so central to life in such a short span of time. For leaders, this should be an exciting time and a particularly exciting opportunity: all you have to do is take advantage of it.

CHAPTER 1

THE THREE PLACES

RECREATING THE SECOND PLACE

There is a concept from sociology that I find myself thinking a lot about these days concerning the various kinds of environments that we surround ourselves with as human beings. The theory was best put forth by Ray Oldenburg in his work *The Great Good Place*, in which he talks about the three different kinds of "places" around which we organize our lives—home, work, and social places. According to Oldenburg, we cultivate distinctions between each of these three places and use the differences between them to both organize and enrich our lives. As someone who has been a remote-work leader for almost a decade now, the combination or intermixing of the first two kinds of places is neither new nor novel. I've done virtual meetings in pajamas, held a

9

conference at my breakfast table, and turned off my camera to take care of an errant child for years now.

The advent of the pandemic, however, has brought about two major changes. Not only has it brought about the collapse of the third place into the first two, but it has also metastasized this collapse to the rest of the world. Almost every company in the world, all the way from Microsoft and Google down to your local grocery store and deli, is having to adapt to a remote-working lifestyle. Additionally, whereas previously people entered into remote-working positions voluntarily and knowing (to some extent) what these positions truly entailed, millions of people now face the prospect of collapsing their work lives into their home lives without really signing up to do so or being prepared for it.

It's important to examine what the word *place* really means in this context. The term doesn't refer simply to a physical environment or location, although it does include that. *Place* also refers to all the minute interactions or "rituals" we have with all the people and objects that make up the different places. At home, we might have rituals that involve only ourselves, like brushing our teeth, sleeping, making ourselves coffee, and watching TV in our pajamas. We also have interactions with others who live in our home, like eating a family dinner, talking with a partner about how the day went, or even taking a dog for a walk. At work, these rituals include a watercooler conversation, a catnap after our lunch break, or that four-hour meeting every Wednesday afternoon. Lastly, we engage in social rituals, which occur outside these two spheres, at bars, clubs, bowling alleys, our kids' soccer games, and other venues.

As leaders, our roles and rituals also change as we move across these different spaces. It doesn't make sense to be the same kind of person in each context. At home we might need to be compassionate and sensitive in a way that might be inappropriate for a workplace. At work we might be goal-oriented and occasionally even blunt or severe with our peers in a way we would never be with our loved ones. In a social setting, the role of a leader might even be to be as invisible as possible—we might just melt away as hosts and let our peers interact with one another. Our different rituals and the ways we adapt them to different places, as leaders and employees, can often go overlooked. We perform them so often—and so unconsciously—that they become the unnoticed undercurrent in our lives.

With the recent mass adoption of remote-working protocols, I find that I can divide my colleagues, regardless of whether they're old hands or new hires, into two convenient piles: those who are happy or comfortable with the change and those who are not. Of the latter, almost all share the belief that remote work is either temporary or something separate from their regular lives, or both. What they also have in common is how they approach rituals: when they moved to remote work from regular work, they entirely abandoned many of their formerly overlooked rituals.

Some colleagues did this because they believed that they would be going back to work soon and didn't need to reorient their rituals to the new normal. Others did it because they never noticed the importance of ritual in their work life and thought of remote work as an entity that was separate from the rest of their lives, a kind of fourth "limbo" place that had nothing to do with the other three. The fact is, however, that not only is remote work here to stay, but it's very much continuous with life. What these colleagues don't realize is that the very abandonment of these rituals is what affects their ability to adapt to the new world. In this chapter, we'll explore the importance of these rituals, how we can take them online, and the role of the leader in doing this.

WHY DO RITUALS MATTER?

As I mentioned briefly above, we perform rituals so often that they can become invisible. Think about some of the things you do in the morning before a regular workday (or that you used to do before all work went remote). You make yourself a cup of coffee or buy one from the coffee shop opposite your office. You flick through the newspaper or get your news from your Twitter feed on the bus or subway ride. You greet the receptionist at the front desk and they ask you how your partner, kids, or nephews are doing. These are all things that are part of every one of our normal workdays, and we do them so often that they become reflexive behaviors, almost like muscle memory. If someone asked you at the end of your day what your day had been like, you would almost always mention either the tasks that you worked on or anything novel, unusual, or exciting that happened. What would get overlooked are the repetitive rituals.

If they're so invisible, why do they matter?

- **Continuity:** Through performing these repetitive rituals, we establish continuity with all the previous days in which those rituals were part of the routine. They tell us that this too is like any other workday, and in doing so, they ground us and remind us of all that we did at work the previous day and all that we need to do today to continue to do well.

- **Structure:** We also build our day around these rituals. They discipline us. Think about how many of your rituals occur at specific times. Everything from your 7 AM morning coffee to your 5 PM. discussion of the previous day's basketball scores with your pickup team from work. We also structure the rest of our day around these rituals. We might choose, for example, to do particularly strenuous work only after something that calms us, like a quick walk around the block. We might also make sure we complete all our high-priority tasks before a ritual that we enjoy, like a weekly lunch with our supervisor.

- **Delineation:** So far, all the examples have involved the workplace, only one of Oldenburg's three distinct environments. However, rituals also serve to delineate and separate the different parts of our lives. We do certain rituals only at work or only in social places and never mix the two (or three) parts of our lives. In doing so, we help separate the goals, stresses, joys, and people involved in all three places and try to avoid associating any emotions or attitudes from one place with another place. As a funny exercise, imagine trying to interact with your colleagues like you do with your friends in a pub. Or worse yet, imagine sitting at your work desk like you might lie on your sofa reading the newspaper in your robe in the morning, legs sprawled, hair disheveled. Some things aren't meant to be mixed, and rituals help keep them separated.

- **Joy:** As I mentioned in one of the examples above, not all rituals are there to serve some greater purpose. Many of them exist simply to keep you content and happy, especially on a particularly tough day. In fact, one of my favorite rituals, and one I perform every day, is making my own tea, because it gives me a small break from my hectic day and is a meditative process in itself. No matter how hard my day is, I will be sure to make myself a cup of tea.

- **Calm and comfort:** Both of these factors are closely related to those discussed above. By giving us structure, rituals provide a sense of order and calm for the brain. Rituals make us feel like our days are just the same as the previous ones and are continuous with them, and help us ensure we don't take our work life home (or to a party) and vice versa.

- **Efficiency:** In the United Kingdom, stressed workers account for more than 50 percent of the working days that are lost per year.[1] That's more than thirteen million lost working days. Rituals give us a common purpose and bind a community closer together. A calm and comfortable worker is also an efficient, innovative, and successful worker.

- **Social dynamics:** Think about how people greet each other. In North America, a hug is common. In some European countries, *la bise*, or the kiss, is customary. In many parts of Asia, just a hello might suffice. It's interesting to see people from different cultures greet each other when they don't know what to do. Social dynamics are the bedrock of our culture, and retaining offline social interactions, such as pre-meeting small talk, is critical for maintaining rituals.

- **Organizational purposes:** Businesses also use rituals to help organize teams and encourage team members to work well with one another. These rituals tend to be team activities that are repeated every week, fortnight, or even month. They can be as simple as five minutes of informal discussion for the engineering team every morning or a Friday-night happy-hour session for the entire HR department.

Rituals not only help create a sense of psychological calm and security for an individual worker, but also help businesses organize themselves and become more efficient. The importance to leaders of engendering these rituals should be obvious given all the purposes they serve (and the list above isn't nearly exhaustive). Remote-working leaders should be motivated to continue to foster ritualized behaviors because these help both the leaders and their employees become far more valuable workers.

Remote leaders should keep in mind, however, that they must actively encourage the development of these rituals, and not take it for granted that their employees either can or will do so of their own accord. Remember the sad colleagues I talked about above? The ones who didn't "love" remote work? Some of them didn't even realize that it was rituals that helped them organize their workday and kept them calm and active. In moving to remote work, they unknowingly abandoned things that were important to them and would have never noticed this until told! By preserving (at least some of) these rituals when moving to a virtual work environment, we also allow them to confer the same benefits they provide in physical environments.

Organizing the workday isn't the only reason why leaders must take the initiative to move rituals online. Employees may be reluctant or shy to speak up about rituals that gave them joy at work. For example, now that you're working on your computer at home all day, how can you have your weekly Friday exercise session at 10 AM with the rest of your team when you aren't even working in the same location anymore? As a leader, you have to remember, notice, and speak up for these employees and their rituals.

TAKING RITUALS ONLINE

In moving from a physical to a virtual work environment and transferring behaviors from one space to another, the first step is to identify what rituals matter to you and your office. This may seem obvious, but it's not. It requires a lot of thought, a lot of digging through memories and notebooks, and a lot of documentation with pen, paper, and planner.

The best way to encourage behaviors you would like to see at work is by practicing them yourself. If there are rituals that you would like to see your employees take online, start by showing them that you do them too! Take your hourly coffee break, even if it's during a four-hour meeting, as long as that's what you used to do in a normal workday. Make sure your workers know that it is both okay and important to take previous and long-held behaviors online.

When I first moved from a physical to a fully virtual work environment in my role as head of international business development at Rohto Pharmaceutical in 2020, I remember immediately noticing the sudden change and loss of certain rituals in my work life, and I took steps to address this.

Here's how I did it:

1. I first looked back through my daily agendas from my previous role to identify all the weekly and other repetitive rituals I used to participate in.

2. I tried to remember what a standard workday looked like for me from the moment I woke up until I walked back in through my front door in the evening.

3. Then, I took an hourly planner and I marked every single event that mattered that I could think of alongside the time that I used to do it every day.

4. After that, I considered other special and rare rituals that occurred for major holidays or birthdays and anniversaries (more on this later) and collated them along with the rest.

5. Finally, I tried to gauge which rituals could and couldn't be transposed onto a virtual workplace, and which rituals could be useful for me and the other employees in the office, and I had a conversation with my supervisor about trying to keep the appropriate rituals alive. Some of my recommendations were accepted and many weren't, but the exercise has stayed with me.

In addition to occasionally practicing this exercise for myself, I also hold sessions with employees to discuss their schedules and rituals, asking them to complete the above exercise for themselves. These sessions help me understand how I can make their transition from a physical to virtual environment as smooth as possible.

Once you've done this exercise with your employees, you will get a sense of what they want, and you can then determine what rituals can, in fact, be moved to a remote-working environment. In doing so, the two factors you have to consider are feasibility and authenticity.

The former might seem self-explanatory. There are some rituals that are simply impossible to bring online. How does a quick workout in the gym across from your office translate when you're working from home?

At the same time, certain rituals that initially appear unfeasible to transpose can actually be easily transferred using novel methods enabled by modern technology. Think about having your weekly work lunch with your most trusted colleagues at that café that you all love. While it might initially seem that remote working denies you the chance to do this, online delivery services now enable all of you to order and receive your food separately, allowing you to preserve this important ritual. Although remote working and the pandemic have taken many rituals away, new technology infrastructures have helped preserve some rituals and have even allowed other new rituals to be created. A leader should always be open to discovering and introducing these new methods, some of which we will explore later in this chapter and in the rest of the book.

An equally important factor in transposing rituals is ensuring that their authenticity is maintained in the process. Rituals that are authentic maintain their value to both employee and leader, convey their benefits to those involved, and are carried out with sincerity just as they were planned.

At first sight, some rituals may entirely lose their ability to be authentic when moved online. These rituals tend to be social in nature, like after-work drinks. Is it really possible to move happy hour online?

I, for one, maintain that it is possible to move rituals online. In fact, at my company I still host one-on-one virtual meetings with my employees to discuss their own visions for their future life, just as I used to do before the pandemic. We call these sessions "vision meetings" and we discuss everything but work.

I believe that if a ritual feels inauthentic online, it also very likely feels inauthentic offline. The secret to maintaining the value of these kinds of events and rituals is having them hosted and organized by people who fundamentally believe in them. Leaders are emulated, and our values and the ways in which we comport ourselves during such online events are contagious. If you would like your employees to take an event seriously, you must do so first.

THE RITUALS

So far, I've been talking about the actual online rituals tangentially, in terms of only the benefits they confer and the ways in which they can be moved online. In this section, I want to talk about some commonly overlooked rituals in the workplace, how they can be transported to a remote-working environment, and how they actually look in practice.

Commuting is an often-overlooked ritual that serves as a dividing space, providing time between home and work. It's a ritual that you might imagine is impossible to move online. The time during our commute—especially if we ride a bus, tram, or train—also serves several other purposes. It can be a time of calm, when we listen to music or our favorite podcast, prepare for the day ahead, or decompress after work. It can be a time of planning, when we review our tasks and goals, and even a time for socialization, when we talk and interact with fellow commuters.

For almost everyone, moving to a remote-working environment will completely eradicate not only commuting time but also the benefits that go along with it. In fact, in a survey by VoxEU of ten thousand American workers, more than 35 percent of the respondents said they allocated the time they saved by not commuting to simply doing more work![2]

Companies like Microsoft, however, have recognized the importance of the commute. Its CEO, Satya Nadella, summed it up himself in an interview: "But one of the big concerns I have, even for myself, is the loss of those transitions in a day. I never thought I would say this, but rituals like a commute are missing; nobody thought they liked their commute, except it's one of those times when you switch off, and those transitions matter."[3]

To combat the loss of the commute, Microsoft introduced a new feature called the "Virtual Commute" to Teams, its online collaboration and conferencing software. The feature provides workers with a meeting-free period before and after work to allow them to transition to and from their home. An app asks users to check off all tasks that they've completed during the day and prompts them to plan ahead for their tasks tomorrow. Virtual Commute also integrates with Headspace, the virtual meditation app, providing workers some calm through guided meditation.

As leaders, we need to be sensitive to basic, overlooked rituals and the potential to bring them online. Social rituals include small talk, meals, tea or coffee breaks, and general office chats that allow us to get to know our coworkers. Work rituals include the collaborative ways in which we work: brainstorming together with Post-it notes, drawing out our thoughts in whiteboard sessions, and holding our morning and midday stand-up meetings.

We can replicate social rituals by creating the space and option for people to socialize. One of the most difficult things about moving social rituals online is that people are not sure if this is acceptable, or they're worried about how they will be perceived if they start such an initiative. Here, leaders can empower and encourage their teams to get creative in developing social outlets, such as a repeating Zoom meeting on Friday for eating together that people can join if they're free, or a social 24/7 Clubhouse channel just for the company's employees. If the company used to have free Friday lunches, it can seek to recreate this ritual by ordering food to be delivered to employees' houses on Fridays and encouraging people to eat in the same digital meeting together.

Similarly, we can also replicate work rituals. In my company, we do morning stand-up meetings, which are quick check-in meetings where everybody stands in a circle. We now have the same meetings scheduled and everybody still stands up! We use live Google Docs and Jamboards to collaborate together so that we can all see our ideas when we don't have physical whiteboards in front of us. We use parts of the meeting for dedicated brainstorming, where we seek to retain the spirit of collaboration and working together in real time.

The interactions mentioned so far are the kind that are repetitive throughout the year and do not involve any special event or holiday. If you think about it, we also modify office rituals for holidays like Christmas, New Year's, and Halloween, as well as special days for individuals like birthdays, anniversaries, and more. Just as people structure and center their days around their minor rituals, so too do they structure entire years and months around these larger, more special days.

My colleagues who didn't want to adapt to remote work insisted on seeing it as something apart from life, its own hermetic environment. But special days like those mentioned above are so important to people that we can't afford to ignore them at work, because work is continuous with the rest of our lives. If celebrations on these days are led by good leaders who desire and value authenticity, then they can be just as enjoyable online as they are in person.

In fact, one of my favorite holidays is Christmas—not just for its cheer and festivity but also because it is such an international holiday. At

Rohto, I oversee five different CEOs and dozens of direct reports working in over twenty different countries. Almost every single one of them celebrates Christmas and takes the initiative to make sure their employees can too. It's not hard to bring to the virtual office a festive cheer during the holiday period. I'm not one for virtual Zoom backgrounds that are Christmas themed. Instead, I might dress up for the day and decorate my work desk at home with appropriate decorations and organize an office-wide secret Santa event in which our employees can send one another gifts virtually. By making the event voluntary, you can also encourage participation from only those who seek authentic experiences.

RITUALS AND THE MIXING OF PLACES

In this final section of the chapter, I want to go back to the notion of "place." As discussed earlier, one of the purposes of rituals is to delineate places. They keep home, work, and social environments separate from one another. For some in the remote-working environment, this may be easy—even though they work remotely, they may still have an office space that they can go to that provides a separate environment. For millions, however, the pandemic has turned their homes into their workplaces. Whereas previously, work rituals were used to delineate work, those rituals are now being brought into the home. It's no longer clear what rituals and interactions are appropriate for which "place," and as leaders we need to be aware of this and learn how to navigate the new normal.

Not everyone has a separate study where they can ensure that work never intrudes into their home and vice versa. Work, as such, can become an intrusion of privacy if a workday is built around virtual meetings that involve cameras and microphones (as most businesses are). As I write this book, I am not only a remote-working leader but also a mother with a child and two pets! While my daughter is old enough to care for herself, I know how easily home life can spill over into work because of my two dogs. It's impossible to work in my tiny study because they consistently bark and scratch at the door. At one point, when I ordered a new office chair, they gnawed at its wheels until it became impossible to use. Given these problems, I choose to work in the kitchen, where I can keep an eye on them. But in my kitchen, intrusions are constant: I'm always dealing with my pups or my daughter, or opening the door for some new package delivery. Given this close acquaintance with the problems of working at home, I'm also sensitive to those faced by my workers.

TAKAKO'S METHODS

Here are some guidelines I keep in mind to help navigate this consolidation of two formerly separate places. My goal in discussing these below is to list some of the means by which leaders can engender trust within their team. In a world where we're now sometimes unable to meet our colleagues in person, leaders need to take extra steps to create the kind of trust that enables workplaces to function effectively.

- Remember, behaviors that you may have previously thought were inappropriate at work are now unavoidable given that people work at home. Many employees are parents (to human children and pets) and may have to attend to other needs, even in the middle of a meeting.

- Being able to see into someone's home involves intimacy. People may have homes that look different from yours and are different from what you may have expected. All the same, a person's home is something that is very close to their heart. When you discuss your employees' home/work environment with them (if you choose to discuss it at all, see below), do so with tact.

- Additionally, this new intimacy may also change the kind of interactions you have with your employees. Small talk is a big part of working at the office, and when we get visual access to people's homes, we may be unconsciously encouraged to engage in small talk beyond the bounds of what is normal. This isn't necessarily a problem—in fact, virtual environments can sometimes encourage a flattening of hierarchy in conversation that is beneficial to all. Nonetheless, be aware of what you discuss with your employees, and ensure that they are comfortable discussing what used to be entirely private matters.

- Virtual meetings occur both one-on-one and in teams. As I mentioned above, this new virtual intimacy may encourage conversations that wouldn't normally happen in a workplace. Leaders must be aware that certain topics they discuss in one-on-one meetings will not be appropriate to bring up in full-team meetings, and that employees expect a certain amount of confidentiality from their leaders when they discuss subjects that they do not want exposed.

- In order to be an effective leader, you need to not only practice these behaviors yourself but also encourage your employees to adopt them. It is one thing to lead through the expectation of emulation, but it is another to create ground rules for employees and virtual interactions using the above guidelines—doing so can lead to healthy and positive benefits for your employees.

CHAPTER 2

TRUST IN THE REMOTE WORKPLACE

HOW DO YOU MAINTAIN RELATIONSHIPS IN A CONSTANTLY MONITORED ENVIRONMENT?

Google has long been renowned as one of the best places to work in the world. Fun offices, great benefits and pay, excellent cafeterias—Hollywood even made a movie about it, *The Internship*. In late 2019, however, Google ordered a Chrome add-on installed on each employee's computer that tracked any invitation sent to more than a hundred people. Google said it created the add-on to fight spam, but what it really wanted to do was prevent employee activism and unionization. This action suggested that Google was actively monitoring its employees, searching through inboxes and messages, and accessing their computer files.

The add-on caused a massive internal row at the company and was the basis for a legal case filed by the US National Labor Relations Board in 2020. Workers thought the add-on opened the door for Google to install more spyware, and they realized they didn't actually have the level of trust and privacy they thought they had. Most importantly, leadership never consulted its employees or asked them for their permission to install the add-on, which caused a growing rift between the monitored and their monitors. The company, whose unofficial new motto at the time was "Do the right thing," had clearly gotten this wrong—and given leaders everywhere a lot to learn from.

The rapid expansion of remote working has forced us, as leaders, to contend with the problem of monitoring, or overmonitoring, our teams. While our employees may no longer be under our physical eye in the office, a plethora of new software and applications means that even when they are working in their homes, perhaps countries and continents away, we can constantly stay in contact with them, monitor their progress on projects, and even look at (or control!) their laptop screens. Think about how many ways you interact with your team now—Zoom, Teams, WhatsApp, WeChat, Weibo, Slack, even Instagram—and how easily you can reach them at any time of the day, if you have to.

At the same time, the distance between workers in remote-working environments means that leaders also have to confront additional problems—those related to our nature as a fundamentally *social* animal.

By "social," I don't mean that all of us necessarily love to fraternize or party—I know I don't! Instead, what I mean is the idea that no humans exist, or even *can* exist, in isolation. We learn how to be ourselves through our interaction with others. Civilization itself was formed on the basis of our interactions and cooperation with one another.

The rapid growth of remote work has undercut our ability to be fundamentally social animals. In moving most, if not all, of our interactions online, we lose many of the micro-interactions cultivated through rituals, as discussed in the previous chapter. Not all interactions can be moved online. Our basic connection with one another has been eroded.

These changes have a dramatic effect on one of the main bedrocks of the workplace and all person-to-person relationships—trust. How can we get our teams to trust us, their leaders, when we are so far away, but still look over their shoulders whenever we want to? Is there a way to find a balance between monitoring our employees too much and ensuring work gets done on time? How can we ensure that our team members trust one another? In this chapter, I will explore why trust is central to the workplace and how we, as leaders, can maintain it in the new remote-working sphere.

THE PURPOSE OF TRUST

Trust has three interrelated components. The first is our sense of expectation: when we trust someone, we have some level of knowledge of their abilities and the ways they normally behave. The second is belief: in addition to knowing their abilities, when we trust someone, we also have confidence that the person will behave in a manner consistent with our knowledge of them. The third is reciprocation: in trusting someone, we also believe that, in return, they have corresponding beliefs and knowledge about us.

When we say that we no longer trust someone, one or more of these components has eroded.

Why is it important not to let the components of trust erode? Because trust is the basis of all our interactions in the workplace or anywhere else. If I have no belief in your abilities, I'm unlikely to want to interact with you at all, because I have no way of predicting how you will behave in that interaction in the first place. This applies to both the expectations a leader has for their team and the expectations a team has for its leader.

What purposes, then, does trust serve in the workplace?

- **Trust is important for morale:** If I'm going to work every day at a place where I neither receive trust nor expect it, I am going to be an unhappy worker. Without trust, we feel isolated and alone, and a team consisting of people feeling alone is no team.

- **Trust is important for communication:** This is perhaps one of the most important roles that trust plays. If I have no trust in my coworkers and leaders, then this is going to affect how I communicate with them. Without trust, I am less likely to want to communicate new ideas, confide fears, or express doubts to my coworkers and team leaders. A lack of honest communication between a team manager and their team is one of the telltale symptoms of a low level of trust.

- **Trust is important for productivity:** As discussed in the previous chapter, the best workers are comfortable workers. In the absence of trust, workers with low morale are less likely to perform as efficiently as possible, thereby affecting the productivity of the office. Communication problems arising from trust issues will also further hamper productivity.

- **Trust is important for leadership:** In order to get the most out of yourself as a leader, you require team members who trust you. Without trust, your own team members will be unable to execute projects in the manner you expect of them, thereby diminishing your own ability to accomplish your goals.

- **Trust is important for results:** As you may have noticed in each of the points above, trust between team members is fundamental to the success of an office. If your workers are unhappy, taciturn, and unproductive, and you are unable to be the leader you believe yourself to be, then you're also going to be in charge of a team or office that is unable to achieve the kind of results that are expected of them by different stakeholders.

In reading the points above, you might notice that there are, in fact, two different kinds of trust. The first is trust between people—both between you and your team and between the members of your team themselves. A solid foundation on this level of trust then automatically engenders a second, far more important kind of trust: a trust in rituals, processes, and working methods.

This kind of trust is organizational trust, whereby the team believes that its common approach is effective and should be adhered to. For example, tech companies might have an agile or scrum work approach to their projects—an established framework that dictates the pace and allocation of work. The rituals surrounding time-tested approaches are important because they are what people are used to. If a leader fails to respect or follow through on such processes, or abandons them altogether, employees can come to distrust that leader.

Barriers to Trust

Some barriers to trust are endemic to both in-person and remote-working offices. A culture of poor communication is a fairly common problem, and it's particularly harmful for office culture because it hampers both our expectations of our coworkers and our confidence in them. In effect, when communication is poor, we're using incomplete sources or even tertiary data to get a sense of who our coworkers are and what they can do for our team.

Encouraging unhealthy competition between team members often creates barriers to healthy communication. A colleague of mine once worked as a reporter at an infamous online news publication in England that I will refrain from naming here. All reporters were told to prioritize garnering "clicks" when choosing what stories to write. Every day, a TV screen in the middle of the newsroom displayed the stories with the most clicks, as well as a leaderboard of the most popular reporters. In turn, those who received the most clicks were also assigned the juiciest stories by their editors. My colleague said it was one of the most harrowing work environments he had ever been in, where reporters did not share useful information with one another, morale was low, and reporters distrusted editors because of the favoritism they showed to certain writers.

Leaders have to take the lead in encouraging a healthy culture of communication, but cannot do so while remaining inscrutable to their employees. If you are the type of leader who hides all your communication, workflow, and decision-making processes from your team, you're encouraging them to trust and communicate with you less. They may perceive you as someone with entirely different beliefs, goals, doubts, and expectations from theirs, further affecting the cohesiveness of your office.

Some managers—and I've worked with them—also believe that a position of power over their team members makes them automatically entitled to trust. This is an entirely false belief. Trust isn't something that exists on its own. Rather, it is something to be formed, nurtured, and practiced with discipline (as you will see below). If you want your team members to trust you and one another, you have to put into place the kind of systems and culture that allow for trust to grow in the first place, and then participate in it yourself.

Some leaders and offices even go so far as to think that trust between themselves and between their teams is entirely unnecessary! These leaders also tend to be aggressive managers, believing that poor office morale is all right, as long as their "team" is achieving results. Workers in these offices might find that they can succeed in an environment where goals are prioritized above all else, but at the cost of any kind of healthy relationship between themselves and their peers.

In addition, leaders with international team members should be wary of treating all their employees in the same manner. As an international remote-working leader, I've noticed that some cultures start with a default base level of trust while others require it to be earned first. In Asian countries, trust must be earned, whereas in the United States, there is a baseline trust already there. As remote work breaks down borders and allows us to work with individuals from other time zones and cultures, we have to think about each culture's default approach to trust and how to best establish it to have a healthy working relationship.

In addition to culture, distance exacerbates trust issues by further affecting communication. When we're no longer face-to-face with our teammates, we lose all the micro-interactions that offer insight into emotional and psychological contexts and make full communication possible. Although we live in a time when there are more modes of communication than ever before, quantity cannot necessarily replace what we've lost qualitatively. If you've ever tried to celebrate a birthday over a group video call, you know what I'm talking about.

There are also barriers to trust that are unique to remote-working and virtual environments. As discussed in the first chapter, we face many new distractions, particularly when working at home. Distractions affect our ability to communicate—think about a Zoom meeting with a distracted colleague. They also affect our productivity and ability to achieve goals on time because we are drawn away to other things that better hold our attention. Virtual work environments also mean we're no longer under the direct and real eye of our superiors, and this may encourage us to put off work that we would have done immediately in the office. When working together in person, we act on the basis of seeing and being seen. When we feel as if the latter may no longer be the case, we may unconsciously or consciously change our behavior because we feel like we're less beholden to our superiors.

Working from home and staring at a computer screen all day can also cause burnout, which affects trust. We know from the first chapter that a stressed worker is also a less productive worker, and leaders may thus trust their teams less because they think distractions are causing a loss in productivity, when in fact the cause is burnout and stress. One Gallup national health study revealed that, compared to before the pandemic, 15 to 20 percent more US adults felt worried and stressed.[1] More significantly, the study found that adults who worked from home were almost always more stressed and worried than those who went out to work. Who knew that looking at a screen all the time would be so tough? On top of that, a Stanford University study showed that more than 13.8 percent of women felt "very" to "extremely" fatigued after videoconference calls, compared to 5.5 percent of men, thanks to the "mirror anxiety" caused by the self-view window.[2]

Finally, we've all witnessed instances when technology breaks down and simply doesn't allow someone to get a point across. It's frustrating for everyone. These situations are inevitable, but can naturally damage our trust in another person's reliability, even if the problem was the technology's fault. Consequently, as will be discussed later, we should troubleshoot and anticipate technical issues in advance in order to prevent a deterioration in trust.

Overmonitoring

When remote-working leaders feel that they're no longer getting what they expect out of team members and no longer have the confidence in those members' ability to deliver results on time, they turn to the primary remedy: monitoring.

Monitoring has always been an essential part of work, both virtual and in person. Leaders use it to keep tabs on their workers and on the progress of their respective projects. With remote working, however, the plethora of monitoring "remedies" has grown dramatically. They include, from least to most invasive:

- **Virtual meetings:** This may be an overlooked category, but meetings are the primary means by which leaders keep

tabs on their team both online and offline. I have check-in
meetings with my teams on Zoom almost every day.

- **Virtual time cards:** Many companies now use an online
  version of time cards to see when employees log in and out of
  their work computers.

- **Checklist software:** Some companies use shared checklist
  applications where employees can check off different
  milestones and upload any material they've completed.
  Leaders can access this material and make sure that goals are
  being completed on time.

- **Office chat:** Applications like Slack, a business-
  communication platform organized around chat rooms that
  are grouped around different teams and topics, allow team
  members to communicate with and update one another
  constantly.

- **Social media tracking:** Many companies now track their
  employees on social media platforms like Twitter and
  Instagram and have rules and norms about what their
  employees can say about their work on social media.

- **Screen timing:** Some companies and leaders use software to
  see how long their employees remain logged in on their work
  computers (this works similarly to virtual time cards).

- **Monitoring emails:** Companies that provide their employees
  with email accounts may also monitor the contents of all
  messages sent between the employees' email IDs on company
  servers. Companies may do so in order to track objectionable

behavior, illegal actions, and any kind of potential loss of proprietary data, among other reasons.

- **Advanced screen logging and keystroke logging:** Some companies go so far as to use software that tracks every single key an employee presses on their work computer at any time of the day. Software also exists that allows team leaders to look at their employees' screens at any given time and see if they're logging time on "productive" software or wasting time.

These methods are growing day by day. One Gartner survey of large companies shows that at least 50 percent of them use "nontraditional" monitoring software, looking at things like emails, social media, whom employees are meeting, and how they are using their workspaces.[3]

When using tracking software, leaders must be careful to strike a balance between trusting their employees too much and too little. Some oversight over work and progress is reasonable. At my company, sales managers track their teams' sales data and the hours they spend in meetings with their clients. This is reasonable.

Leaders should be wary of straying into the territory of too much monitoring. Team members can feel like monitoring is an unnecessary and inexcusable intrusion into their private lives and they may feel like they are being babied by their supervisors, as if they cannot innovate and progress on their own but instead need constant supervision.

Overmonitoring can also make team members doubtful of their own abilities. If my boss keeps checking on me constantly for no (apparent) reason, I may begin to worry that I don't have the ability to do the work on my own. Too much intrusion may also lead me to believe that I'm being checked on because I'm not completing my goals on time, even when that might not be the case. As a leader, you don't want to check on your team too much or give them excessive advice. You risk antagonizing them by making it seem like only you know the correct solution to every problem.

Solving Trust Issues

The mistake many remote-working leaders make is trying to solve the wrong set of problems. Instead of addressing those that are common to both virtual and real environments, they focus on those that are specific to virtual ones.

It's not hard to see why. Commercial monitoring solutions present leaders with a simple economic equation—pay me X amount of money for my software and I will generate Y amount of returns for your team and company. And by turning a leadership problem into a contractor problem, leaders can remove themselves from the equation. The problem with this attitude is that it overlooks the very people that form a company. This easy way out will exacerbate the problem it's trying to solve by hindering trust.

When team members communicate well with one another and their leaders, when their morale is high, and when they believe in their work and the processes used to meet goals, problems like distractions and procrastination are almost irrelevant. Motivated employees are also unlikely to have problems with burnout, simply because they're invested in their work.

The solutions to trust issues in remote-working environments are more intuitive than you would imagine and center on a number of factors, including:

- **Communication:** To maintain trust between you and your team, you need to ensure that your communication is frequent and, more importantly, meaningful. Meaningful communication not only deals with the specifics of work but is attuned to the needs and goals of your team members themselves. The primary way you can communicate with your team is through feedback.

- **Feedback:** In the Gallup poll cited above, the remote workers surveyed said that a key factor in keeping them engaged at work was feedback; the more feedback remote workers receive, the more engaged they feel. When you, as a leader, provide meaningful feedback to a team member, you show them three things: (1) that you understand that the goal of your relationship is continuous improvement, wherein they can become a better version of themselves; (2) that you care about not only the company's performance and well-being but also theirs; and (3) that you and your team are invested in each other's success, not just your own.

- **Inclusion:** Practice including your team members in the decision-making and leadership process as much as possible. This may be something as simple as having a rotational policy in which a member of your team leads your daily discussion, or even allowing team members to bring in their own proposals for projects. This will give your team the ability to pursue future goals with confidence.

- **Shared control:** Trust works two ways. Both parties must give it, earn it, and maintain it. This means that employees should have a say in how they would like to build trust. This might include:

- allowing team members to give constant and upwards feedback, grouped anonymously if needed.

- encouraging teams to have informal discussion sessions with one another and allowing them to have private means of communication where they can discuss their work and your leadership without your interference.

- **Investment:** At Rohto, we have a culture of encouraging employees to seek other opportunities for work outside their tasks at Rohto. In fact, I spend three to four days a month consulting for Morisawa, a historic typographical company based in Osaka. The idea behind this is that workers gain new knowledge by working for companies with different cultures, goals, and workflows, and they then bring those novel ideas back to Rohto. As long as a worker is completing tasks on time, we don't mind if they take a few days off every month to pursue other interests.

- **Transparency:** As a leader, you have far more access to the lives and work of your team members than they have to yours. To fix this imbalance, make yourself as accountable to your team as the team is to you. Give them insights into your work process; tell them about your doubts and fears, and also your greatest goals and expectations.

- **Freedom through accountability:** Make it clear to your employees that they are accountable for completing specific goals, and do not micromanage them in that process. By being transparent about what team members are accountable for, what you are responsible for, and what your goals are, you give your team room to achieve your joint goals with creativity and freedom. In managing my international teams, in particular, I make sure to give them a long leash in terms of choosing the sales strategies they would like to pursue, even if they go against my best instincts. I then check in on the teams' sales about every two months, rather than hovering over them every day or week. They almost always reward my trust with excellent growth.

- **Balanced relationships:** The final key to maintaining trust with your team is to create and maintain balanced interpersonal relationships. Your team members aren't your best friends, but neither are they your inmates. If you treat them with the amount of care and trust that is appropriate to the workplace, they will return the favor. Even though humans may have a natural tendency to trust one another, what's more important is the ability to share more personal issues or feelings about issues, which takes courage. This means that your teammates may be hesitant to share things with you unless you first open up to the team.

Before I move on to my methods, I want to return to Google. While the spyware case may still be ongoing as I write this, Google recently launched several new features as part of Workspace, its set of collaboration and productivity applications, in response to the growing adoption of remote work. One of those new tools is Time Insight, which automatically collates, analyzes, and then presents employees with data about their productivity and the amount of time they spend in meetings. These data are not available to the employees' superiors (unless employees choose to share it) and can be used to improve time management.

I mention this tool because it takes what has traditionally been a manager's monitoring tool (looking at employees' meeting data), makes it private, and then empowers team members to make their own decisions about time management rather than having a superior tell them what to do. Google is apparently learning that trust is essential to the remote-working environment, and hopefully so will their millions of corporate users.

TAKAKO'S METHODS

Over the years, I've also developed some of my own methods to help build trust in remote teams. They are simple, but effective:

- Host a meeting with your team and ask each member to write down a definition of trust. Have everyone share their written definitions. Discuss their definitions and see if your team can then work together to write a common definition. Then pin it somewhere visible like in a Slack channel.

- Remove any mechanisms at work that monitor whether an employee is online or working. Trust is something that should be assumed to be there, and each time the team meets or surpasses expectations, that trust is built upon. Employers violate their employees' trust when they use software that tracks their screens or keyboards.

- Recognition is one of the strongest motivators at work and helps ensure that leaders and employees are paying attention to their colleagues' results and execution. Host a "snaps" session every two weeks where you collect anonymous compliments or statements of gratitude from teammates about other people in the organization. In the larger team meeting, read out these anonymous snaps that praise or give thanks.

- Periodically in a group chat, ask how others' energy levels are, on a scale of zero to 100 percent. Foster a culture that allows people to report zero, if they wish. This exercise is meant to show that we are all human. None of us can always be at high energy or in a good mood, and we all have varying levels of focus and energy at different hours. This allows teammates to trust that even if they are feeling down, they can make up for their lack of energy later.

CHAPTER 3

FORMS OF COMMUNICATION IN THE REMOTE WORLD

YOU HAVE ONE NEW MESSAGE

In a physical office, most of our interactions are synchronous. You say hi to a colleague and they say hi back. You walk into a supervisor's office to get approval to begin a new project and receive an answer immediately. You don't understand how the office's new Wi-Fi mesh network works, so your take your laptop to IT to get back online. All of these interactions are synchronous in that they demand responses that are immediate.

Alternatively, we use asynchronous communication all the time. Email, for example, doesn't always require immediate responses. GitHub, an online repository and collaboration tool for open-source software and a subsidiary of Microsoft, builds its corporate culture and goals around being asynchronous. Parts of projects are distributed to individual workers in a manner that allows them to complete their tasks without the need for constant communication with others. Goals and output are prioritized over inputs and questions from supervisors. Asynchronous work allows teams to relax and focus on the work at hand without constant interruption. It also allows remote workers the freedom to complete tasks in their own way, while also taking care of other priorities at home if they need to—like looking after a child, for example.

This kind of system works for GitHub because the company has, over the years, built products and a corporate culture that revolve around the idea of open source. Think Wikipedia, where multiple users can freely collaborate in the creation of an article, each producing some small part remotely, with crowdsourced editing and fact-checking. A majority of GitHub's hires come from backgrounds in open-source work, making them particularly attuned to its culture of communication.

This system of total asynchronous communication may not work for all, but remote-working leaders can learn a lot from GitHub. The company has attuned its workflow to best suit not only its employees but also its products—collaborative software. In this chapter, I'll examine the different kinds of communication tools available to remote leaders and how they can go about choosing the most appropriate methods for their individual teams and workflows.

LOSING SYNCHRONICITY

In the last two chapters, I've talked about how the shift to remote work led to a loss of important parts of communication, but I haven't yet discussed the mechanism by which they were lost. When we think of in-person communication, we don't necessarily think of it containing any information beyond what is expressed verbally. When we give instructions to someone face-to face, for example, the only apparent information conveyed is the content of the instructions themselves.

That isn't entirely true, however. Tone, emotions, and facial expressions all play a very important part in communication as forms of information themselves. In moving to a remote-working environment, we lose these pieces of direct information, and this can cause problems. Here's an example: When you're giving a colleague complex instructions for a project, they may sometimes say they understand what they need to do, even when they really don't. Something in their expression and the tone in which they answer you tells you that they do not fully understand, and you then clarify and simplify your instructions before your team member begins their task.

Now imagine this interaction over email. After you send your instructions, your team member simply responds with a "Yes, I'll get on it," without conveying to you their doubt through their (now absent) tone. As a result, they might complete a task inefficiently or, worse, incorrectly, leading to an undesirable outcome.

When we move from an office to a remote environment, the reduction in in-person interactions doesn't also mean a concomitant decrease in synchronous interactions; if anything, the ratio is *now* the opposite. Between WhatsApp, smartphones, Slack, and Zoom, we already have several different forms of communication that demand immediate responses with their (often infuriating) notification sounds. But although this cacophony is useful in maintaining constant contact (as we will see later in the chapter), it may also hamper communication.

So the number of synchronous interactions isn't necessarily decreasing when we leave our physical offices, because the plethora of new apps makes up for the number of lost physical interactions. What we're losing, however, is the amount of information contained within in-person interactions. Apps can, to some extent, make up for this loss, but only if we use them correctly and to their strengths, restricting the use of each different program to the kind of communication that is most appropriate to it.

THE NEW KINDS OF COMMUNICATION

Before the explosion of remote work, for decades email was our default way of connecting with others in the office. The nature of the medium was such that we could take our time with replies and prepare and structure our thoughts in longer form, often while using all the excuses we could think of for replying to emails late (or not at all). Emails are similar to snail mail in their lack of immediacy.

With the advent of more synchronous "instant messaging"–style communication, however, things have been thrown into some disarray. We feel pressed to reply almost immediately, as if a presence on the other end demands our response. The user interfaces of these applications are set up for us to fire off our thoughts quickly in response; we can even see when others are writing a message or are active online. Meanwhile, red notifications push us to see new developments on a topic. It's these little mechanisms that allow these platforms to mirror a real conversation more closely, in real time, and make the dynamics of remote work possible. These collaborative suites—which I like to call "digital workspaces"—are simply a nonnegotiable requirement for any remote company to succeed.

This is all to say that technology companies have created niche products that email cannot compete with. Slack channels and group chats (both private and public) within a company's greater digital workspace can become microcommunities dedicated to specific projects, interests, or domains. Digital spaces where anyone can chime in and where thoughts and ideas are always being shared make the dynamics spontaneous and lively. When I'm on Slack or Teams, it feels like there are always unread messages and exciting articles being shared. These digital workspaces also naturally build alignment—everyone knows what everyone else is working on, who needs what, and the issues that someone might be facing. They make being on the same page possible without an explicit email and without the need for a formal, time-sucking meeting. Email has no chance in comparison with these real-time platforms.

VISUAL COLLABORATION

While digital workspaces are important in that they bring the workplace online and create a sense of community, there is another critical aspect of remote work that must similarly be brought online. This is project management.

Just as we used to have whiteboards and corkboards where we could write notes or put up Post-its indicating key deadlines and timelines, employees in online workspaces also need to visualize projects from a common viewpoint. Many companies offer solutions in this booming space of project management platforms. Here's a quick primer on what they are and which ones might suit your team best.

For free options, three of my top picks are Airtable, Asana, and Trello, the last of which might be the simplest to start with. For paid options, I recommend Basecamp, Microsoft Project, and Smartsheet, the first of which I find the most intuitive to use. For any kind of new software, there's almost always a small ramp-up period to become familiar with how to use it, and I've found that the best way is to jump right in and click around and input a few test projects and tasks. The occasional YouTube tutorial may help, but once you get the hang of actually using the software with your team, the niche uses will come naturally.

Project management tools help turn individual to-dos into team to-dos. This helps remote leaders sort and prioritize tasks and deadlines, and then communicate the priorities clearly and visually to their teams. One tip here is to have your team members add items into the platform, rather than upload them all yourself. This promotes a sense of ownership and mutual responsibility within the team, because the to-dos do not trickle down from the top. Rather, they are organically suggested by everyone.

Another key aspect of these apps is progress tracking. Seeing items move across different phases of progress and seeing things being checked off (or a growing "finished" list) can instill a sense of accomplishment. This sense of progress is critical for a team, especially one scattered across different locations, because it helps members feel like they're doing tangible work toward a goal.

When you introduce new programs that change your workflow or bring in new hires who may not be familiar with the programs you use, make sure that you have a set of instructions or guides on how to correctly use the app or software. I like to crowdsource guides and tips from my team members to put into a collaborative how-to document, and also organize occasional training sessions with in-house experts.

STREAMLINING COMMUNICATION

The growing adoption of remote work across the globe means that the aforementioned apps are also getting smarter with each new iteration and can be used to make your office even more efficient than it was before adopting a remote environment. At the same time, however, new programs and their concomitant software, notifications, and noises can also create a risk of drowning your teams and office in sheer noise *if* you don't use them correctly.

The first step in using new forms of communications correctly is determining when everyone in your office is available to be trained. As an international leader, I am used to having meetings with my US team and Japanese team at opposite ends of the day. Even if you aren't leading across continents, it's still possible that as a remote leader you will have teams working in different time zones. Collaborative calendar tools make it easy to determine availability, but leaders should also keep time differences in mind. Try not to schedule meetings with team members at times that are inconvenient for them. A 5:30 AM meeting is unlikely to get you their best and most productive selves.

You then need to list all the different kinds of programs your office uses to communicate (including any new kinds you would like to introduce) and match each of them with the most appropriate kinds of communication. Virtual meetings are best used for brainstorming sessions and planning for future tasks and goals, interactions that require instantaneous ideas and spontaneity from your team. They allow you to see the reactions of all your team members to any proposals or new ideas at once (if using video), and new tools like polls and virtual whiteboards allow for the collection of even more information than an in-person meeting does.

Other synchronous communication software like Slack or other messengers is best used to answer questions and address doubts about tasks that are ongoing, and they can also be used for conversations that may not be pertinent to immediate tasks.

Emails, on the other hand, can be used for a mix of synchronous and asynchronous tasks. They should be used for things like action items and formal requests. Emails are more discrete and searchable than chats, so if you're sending information that you know you're going to need at some point in the future, consider using an email.

Tools like collaborative suites and other project management tools should be used for asynchronous communication that doesn't require quick responses. Any time your tasks are progressing smoothly or you, as a leader, need to monitor the progress of a task, online collaborative tools let you provide updates and view those of your team.

By determining what goes where in collaborative tools, you help reduce bloat: you ensure that you and your team know where to look for specific pieces of information, and remove communication from avenues in which it does not belong. The next step is to create a set of guidelines for overall office communication and for each individual medium, in order to solidify and disseminate changes in communication tools throughout your team.

Overall guidelines will determine when it is appropriate to contact a coworker for regular work, under what circumstances it is okay to contact others outside regular hours, how to restrict interactions to the bare minimum, what interactions are appropriate to each medium, and what kind of interactions are banned or discouraged on official company devices, if any. For individual media, some of the guidelines for all team members might look like this:

- **Email:** Institute company-wide standards for subject lines ("NEEDS RESPONSE," for example), and determine what kind of approvals can be made in emails and what kind must be made in person.

- **Slack:** If you have specific questions or concerns that you need answered or addressed, tag the person in question with an @ followed by their name, and then enter the text of the question immediately after. To save time, avoid unnecessary introductions like "Hey" or "How is it going?"

- **Collaborative tools:** Any time you mark a specific task or portion of a task as completed, upload the file or document associated with the task.

- **Zoom:** Determine when and in what kind of meetings it's necessary for team members to have their cameras turned on. Always ensure that meeting agendas are sent out well before they're scheduled to begin.

INFORMAL COMMUNICATION

Earlier in the book, I talked about how the loss of in-person interactions like watercooler moments or spontaneous discussions can lead to a loss of deeper relationships between team members and leaders. As the *MIT Sloan Management Review* reports, the loss of these informal interactions can also affect a company's ability to innovate:

> *To innovate, leaders need to be exposed to new ideas from every level of the organization and shepherd the most promising ones to success. Previously, copresence in the office or routine trips to remote offices enabled employees to form myriad personal relationships and to participate in spontaneous micro-engagements that supported each step of the innovation journey.*[1]

In order to replace these interactions, remote-working leaders have to do something that's a little unintuitive: they have to begin *formalizing* informal interactions. What does this mean? Let me explain it with an example from my own career.

When I joined Rohto, one of my primary assignments was boosting international sales by increasing the interaction between our international teams. At the time, each of our regional teams worked in a siloed manner. They worried about their own products, their own marketing strategies, and their own sales. My job was to forge meaningful connections between them and to get them to share their knowledge with one another.

My first and most important step was to get the separate CEOs to interact. I hosted several informal meetings where they could discuss almost any problem, solution, or idea with one another, meetings in which my moderation and involvement were minimal beyond my presence. Together, almost on their own, the CEOs began to realize that they could implement the ideas of their counterparts in their own markets, and they even started to come up with ideas for new products and transnational marketing campaigns on their own. Needless to say, their efforts have now considerably boosted Rohto's international presence.

Formalizing informal decisions means marking off specific chunks of the working day for your team members to discuss their work, and even their nonwork life, in a more casual manner. This can include team-wide meetings or even one-on-ones between you and your team members. There are many forms that these meetings can take: they can be scheduled as "innovation meetings" at the same time every week; they can be scheduled for the hour or half hour before other, regular meetings; or you can even create a voluntary system whereby your team members can schedule these meetings on their own volition with or without you. Almost needless to say, these meetings should occur over video or audio calls because they require the spontaneity that these communication methods provide.

TAKAKO'S METHODS

Below are some best practices for streamlining communication in a virtual work environment:

- I always make notes before a meeting. They help me think about the things I need to say, the questions I need to ask, and the discussions I need to facilitate. Since beginning remote work, however, I've also started to encourage my team members to create collaborative documents *before* a meeting. When possible, these documents are usually created at least a whole day before the meeting. Together, the team enters content into and organizes the document. During the actual meeting, we throw the document onto a screen (when possible) and it evolves as questions arise, discussions occur, and new tasks are created. Rather than taking individual meeting notes, we create a document that fosters the kind of cross-pollination that is vital to innovation.

- My company makes a lot of use of open Slack channels. These channels are usually arranged thematically—some for formal considerations and others for informal discussions— and contain a mix of lower-level employees, managers, and upper management. This creates a level playing field where team members can interact with their leaders and encourages an office-wide bonhomie that is conducive to trust and productivity.

- As a leader, I don't necessarily believe all synchronous meetings have to be over video. There are several kinds of meetings for which I know beforehand that I don't require the information or interactions provided in a full video call. Before you host any video meetings, ask yourself whether it might be sufficient to have workers on a call over audio only. Remember, many people work from home and video might require extra effort when none is really needed.

- Remember those times in college when you and your roommate or best friend would spend hours together, late at night, studying for an exam or doing an assignment? We all did this at some point. You didn't have to be working on the same project—what really mattered was the presence of someone else working with you. I like to preserve this feeling in my remote-working environment. To do so, I create open video working spaces that employees can voluntarily join at any time during the workweek. These are informal spaces where employees don't really have to be working on the same project together; instead, they benefit from the presence of fellow workers and can interact causally with one another when taking a break from their tasks.

- Even as we move away from offices, I still encourage daily morning stand-up meetings with my teams. If you aren't familiar with the concept, a stand-up meeting is a short meeting in which each team member talks about the project they are working on, their current progress, whether and where they are stuck, and what they are going to work on in the coming days. The name comes from the idea that the meeting should be short enough to be completed while everyone can stand comfortably. I find these meetings energizing and have my team members stand up every morning, even if we're all divided by screens.

- At Rohto, I also encourage my fellow leaders and team managers to host open office-hour sessions. Managers can post these sessions on their collaborative profiles and calendars, and team members can call in at any time during these scheduled hours to have a one-on-one meeting with their leaders. Here, they can ask questions in private, give and request feedback, and talk about matters that aren't suited to group video calls. For leaders, this can also signal their availability and convey that they're willing to listen to their team members.

CHAPTER 4

REINVESTING YOUR SAVINGS

YOUR PRIMARY RESOURCE IS YOUR PEOPLE

In October 2017, the tech company Dropbox signed what was at the time touted as the "largest office lease in San Francisco history."[1] The space was to become its new headquarters, where its employees would be housed in a facility with over 736,000 square feet of floor space—roughly the same area as fifteen American football fields. The deal made some sense at the time. Business was booming at the San Francisco–based cloud computing and storage startup. Its user base was expanding at an explosive rate, it had just raised a new $600 million line of credit, it was preparing for an IPO in the coming months, and it had nearly two thousand employees (who all clearly needed some office space!).

Almost exactly three years later, in the midst of the pandemic in 2020, Dropbox announced on its website its new policy of "Virtual First." Henceforth, almost all day-to-day work and activities of Dropbox employees would be through remote offices. In order to provide some data-based backing for its decision, the company hired the Economist Intelligence Unit, a global business-intelligence company run by the eponymous magazine, to conduct a study of the feasibility of shifting to an almost entirely remote system. The study found that workers in remote environments were "more focused at home and just as engaged as before," while an internal survey by Dropbox showed that nearly 90 percent of its employees did not want to return to "a rigid five-day in-office workweek."[2]

The statement said that this shift not only would allow the company to explore more "enlightened" ways of working, but also would give it the impetus to create better products for its users, who would also be shifting to a new remote-working environment. In-person interactions would not be done away with completely, to be sure. Dropbox would still lease some spaces and call them "Dropbox Studios." All employees would have access to these studios, but with one caveat: "Dropbox Studios will be specifically for collaboration and community-building, and employees will not be able to use them for solo work." The company also announced that it would facilitate "non-linear" workdays (also known as asynchronous work culture), as well as offer a raft of resources to help employees adapt to the new virtual workplace.

This was a big step. Dropbox was not just announcing that it would be moving to remote work in order to protect its employees' health temporarily. Instead, Dropbox was announcing a leap into the unknown, a new form of work in which the very notion of "remote" would come to define the company's work culture. To many, it probably did not come as a surprise that Dropbox was one of the first major companies to announce such a dramatic shift; after all, Dropbox's own cloud-computing products have themselves been partially responsible for the proliferation of remote-working capabilities.

The move was also a shrewd way to save some money. Dropbox was one among many companies that realized that they could, in fact, function just as well *without* a main office as they did with one. In fact, in February 2021 the company announced that it would begin to sublease some of its existing office space to other companies. This makes sense when you consider that office space in San Francisco costs about $13,032 per year per employee. You can probably bet that Dropbox regrets its absolutely enormous lease from 2017.

To be clear, Dropbox's transition to a remote-first environment wasn't entirely smooth. Like several other companies, Dropbox had to lay off over three hundred employees and the COO had to step down. In explaining the decisions to his team, CEO Drew Houston said that Dropbox would now "focus on initiatives that align tightly with our strategic priorities . . . [with] the discipline to pull back from those that don't" and that "Virtual First policy means we require fewer resources to support our in-office environment, so we're scaling back that investment and redeploying those resources to drive our ambitious product roadmap."[3] These changes were implemented not as a response to a dramatic drop in revenue, but rather as part of a new company road map.

The sudden transition to remote work has been rough and unpredictable for many, but the world of remote work offers several advantages for those who are willing to look for them. The shift away from physical offices provides many opportunities for savings beyond just real estate, as we will explore in this chapter. But more savings aren't necessarily an advantage to your company unless you know how to use them correctly. As a leader, you have the responsibility to make sure you don't simply sit pretty with these savings, but instead direct them toward their best and most efficient use. That involves investing further in your number one asset: your teams.

MORE SAVINGS

Regardless of whether your company is moving to an entirely remote-based workplace or a hybrid workplace with a mix of virtual and physical offices, the square footage you're going to need in order to have a place for your teams is going to be dramatically reduced. In addition to saving you money on rent, this also helps you reduce your costs in real estate taxes and overheads like energy costs or cleaning and upkeep services. You may also no longer need the kind of administrative staff hired solely to oversee the running of a physical office. To go a step further, you could even consider subleasing some office space for an additional stream of revenue, like Dropbox did.

The companies where I've worked usually subsidize the travel costs of their employees. This includes daily travel permits for employees commuting by train, late-night taxis for employees working late, and (much more expensive) air travel—nationally and internationally—for managers and administration. If you work with an international team, you know that international travel costs are particularly high and that remote working has almost helped do away with them entirely.

There are also other savings associated with the work lives of your employees. You may no longer need to spend money on providing subsidized food if your company had a cafeteria. Money spent on entertaining your employees through social events like happy hour may also no longer be necessary. You could institute an asynchronous work schedule in which your team doesn't need to be on call or "on the clock" all the time, thereby also saving you a lot of money on overtime. There are also potential savings to be had if you're no longer spending on new office equipment or repairing the printer that has conked out for the eighth time this year. Savings can be found with new hires too. You may no longer need to fly them to your city for interviews, and relocation costs are meaningless because they can simply work from home.

So far, I've largely been talking about tangible, monetary savings. There are also savings associated with an asset that is just as valuable: time. Several studies, like one from a researcher at Stanford, show that employees who work from home are far more productive—almost as much as 13 percent more—than their counterparts in an office.[4] Workers at home are less likely to encounter distractions than office workers are, and are thus able to more conveniently enter periods of focus. Further, with workers no longer spending time commuting to and from work, getting themselves dressed and prepared for the day, and idling some time away with fellow coworkers, there's more time for them to spend actually working—and as we saw in chapter one, this is often exactly what workers end up doing with the extra time they receive when switching to remote work.

However, just because you, as a leader, can save doesn't necessarily mean you should. Your role is to know when to cut back and when not to. For example, as we saw in chapter one, social rituals are very important and you have to figure out ways of taking them online. When you can't do a happy hour in person, it doesn't mean there aren't ways of doing it online. Similarly, no longer serving free or subsidized meals in an office cafeteria doesn't necessarily mean you stop providing your team with them—there are a plethora of apps that will allow you to deliver meals to your employees, or you can give them a budget to order their own meals. In addition, in situations where your employees have more time to work, it doesn't mean they should work more—high productivity at the cost of their comfort and peace of mind will end up being a drain on all of you.

You want your savings to work *for* you, rather than just have them sitting there on your balance sheet. This lets you magnify their value, providing your organization with longer-term benefits. As we'll see below, investing in your team is a great way to add more value to your company, and there are several ways to do so.

WHY DOES REINVESTING MATTER?

Anyone who worked through the pandemic, leaders and team members alike, will remember it as a time of great uncertainty and unpredictability. In addition to the worldwide health and economic catastrophe, the rapidity with which small and large companies had to undergo dramatic changes to their corporate structures left many bewildered. The virus necessitated a dramatic change in how people conceived of work; many workers were confused and feared for their employment.

In that kind of atmosphere, investing in your employees is vital as a sign of trust. It plays the very simple role of telling them that they (still) matter and that your organization is not going to leave them by the wayside as it makes its transition.

At the same time, reinvesting your savings from switching to remote work is just as important in regular times, when there is no crisis, for a variety of reasons:

- Reinvesting your company savings in home-office equipment for your workers is a win-win. It saves them from having to spend their own money, while also helping you increase your team's productivity. When team members have a part of their home or specific equipment devoted solely to work, they can create an "area of focus" at home where distractions are minimized, allowing for periods of deep concentration and greater productivity. Going a step further and investing in technological equipment like the latest routers or portable 5G internet dongles will also ensure that there are no connectivity issues for you and your team.

- Using your savings to invest in new skills and training for your team will also confer long-term benefits to your company. The pandemic and the explosion of remote work have meant that our understanding of companies and what "regular" work culture looks like is changing by the second. Employees with new skills are adaptable to these changes and can help make your team and company more adaptable as a whole. It's easy to look at all the change wrought by the pandemic, sit back, and think, "Well, that's it then. That's all the change that can happen." But we should know by now that this isn't true. Changes are going to continue happening more rapidly than ever, and you want to be part of a company and team that is quick on its feet.

- Upskilling your employees also helps you look to the future. It makes you think about your needs and where you see your company going years from the present. Investing in your employees not only makes them more loyal (see below) but also makes them more promotable. Instead of having to look outside your company to hire for leadership positions—an expensive and time-consuming process—you can begin to train your employees with a view to having them occupy those positions in the future.

- All of the actions described above help make your team members feel like they're "seen" by management. In a remote-working environment where your team members sit miles (or perhaps even states or countries) away from their coworkers and supervisors, they can start to feel isolated and like cogs in a much larger machine that has forgotten about their existence. If savings don't make their way to your team members, they might even come to believe that you prioritize savings or the existence of your organization over their contributions and presence. Reinvesting in them reminds them that they are more than just cogs—they are the lifeblood of your company.

- Reinvesting savings in your employees also encourages them to be more loyal by convincing them that they are vital to the mission of your business. This applies to remote workers as much as it does to office workers, and is crucial for several reasons. We already know that satisfied and happy employees are more productive than disgruntled ones. Furthermore, it is expensive to search for and hire new workers, so retention should be thought of as directly related to your company's financial interests. If your company reinvests its savings to reskill or upskill its employees, then the company will also begin to gain a reputation as one that rewards loyalty and keeps its employees happy. This kind of reputation is vital to attract new talent, especially in the age of widespread remote work. More than ever before, talented workers and graduates are able to pick where they want to work, given that remote working means they're no longer as restricted in terms of both location and the time they need to spend at work. Additionally, a reputation as a supportive company also helps you attract the *right* kind of talent—team members who continually seek to improve or upskill themselves.

CHANNELING REINVESTMENT

As a leader, you will have to take an active role in getting your organization to reinvest its savings into your teams. The first step will involve speaking to your admin and HR teams to determine just how much money *can* be reinvested and how much can be reasonably earmarked for avenues that match your goals.

Once you've determined these amounts, you then need to create a hierarchy of different avenues for reinvestment based on their potential value to your teams. Your first priority should be needs that are absolutely vital to both the functioning and cohesiveness of your office. This could mean investing in home-office equipment and adequate tools for team members who don't have them or using the money toward training that will allow your team to use new equipment in the first place.

This decision-making process has to occur alongside planning for the company's future. Determining goals in advance will also help you create a better hierarchy of needs, including what you will need to meet these goals, who on your team will need to take on new roles, and the kind of investment they will need. Once the more vital needs have had funds earmarked for them, you can move on to the less vital avenues of reinvestment, like replacing the "fun" or social rituals that have been lost in moving to remote work.

TAKAKO'S METHODS

The growth of digital resources and new means of communication alongside remote work means that leaders have access to a whole host of ways to invest in their employees. Here are some of the different methods that I've used in my time as a remote leader:

- **Upskilling:** Between YouTube, LinkedIn, and even Khan Academy, there are likely a million different *free* resources for your employees to learn valuable skills. The problem, however, is that the abundance and variety of resources make them difficult to parse and use efficiently. To help your team make the most of free resources, take the time to create an internal register of useful resources. Organize them thematically, create a guide to accessing the resources, and make sure to write summaries that explain how to use the website involved and who or what skills it's best for.

One way to give team members access to paid education opportunities is to provide them with a monthly "skilling" budget that offers the opportunity to use company funds toward learning whatever they'd like. The problem with this method is fairly obvious: your team members may not be learning skills that are useful to your company or to its future, and a budget alone doesn't solve the problem of parsing through millions of different online resources.

You can solve both of these problems by negotiating a deal with a website like Udemy and giving your employees institutional access to paid courses on that website. This way, *you* can choose content that is relevant and of the highest quality, while also giving your team members some leeway in terms of what they want to learn.

- **Corporate training:** Working remotely doesn't mean you have to do away with on-site training programs in management and leadership. Corporate-learning organizations offer the same syllabi for remote-working companies as they do for in-office companies. These programs can easily be organized over several Zoom sessions and use virtual collaborative tools to great effect.

- **Subsidized education:** Almost all the organizations I have worked for offer team members grants or scholarships for further study if the employee commits to returning for a fixed amount of time after completing their education. The cost of the subsidy is easily outweighed by the new skills and learning they bring back, as well as the money saved in assigning them leadership positions instead of hiring or looking for someone outside the organization. In return, you receive a teammate who is loyal, has a vision of the future that aligns with your own, and is interested in continually bettering themselves.

- **Subscriptions:** Institutional subscriptions to publications are another way to ensure you work with a team that keeps abreast of the latest news and trends in business. This can include subscriptions to leading newspapers, business publications, trade publications in your specific industry, or even informative magazines that aren't as relevant to your industry yet help broaden your team's perspective. You may no longer have piles of the *Financial Times* or *NYT* lying at the entrance to your office, but you can still make sure your team has access.

- **Physical and mental health:** The best managers and leaders know that the physical and mental well-being of their teams correlates directly to the productivity and overall cohesiveness of their offices. (This also explains why several large organizations—banks and tech startups alike—have gyms in their offices.) There is a spectrum of ways to help encourage your employees to live healthier lives, from small, physical tools like blue-light glasses to protect their eyes and help them sleep better; to access to mental health resources and counselors; to passes to their local gym. These resources and the need for them will be discussed at length in the following chapter.

- **WFH fund:** You should also consider creating a work-from-home fund for your team. This will help subsidize the creation of home-office spaces for your employees that help them with their focus and their productivity. This can include providing them with technology like Wi-Fi or computers or more simple support like comfortable working chairs, headphones, and mics.

- **Overtime meals:** Even after some companies moved to a remote environment, they've continued to provide team members who work overtime with free meals, just as if they're spending a late night at the office. In order to do so, you can either create a corporate account that your employees can charge their meals to directly or create a system whereby employees pay for their meals themselves and then receive a reimbursement at the end of the month. It's a great reminder to your team that you are sensitive to their hours even if everyone is not working in the same office.

- **Additional assistance:** Reinvesting can also simply mean providing support for employees in stages of life that require additional assistance. Your team members can be going through a pregnancy, grieving, or facing some other big life change, and providing them with the tools or means to help navigate their new path in life is also an investment. It helps engender loyalty to you and the company, creating a desire in your team to repay the favor.

CHAPTER 5

MENTAL HEALTH IN THE REMOTE WORKPLACE

HOW ARE YOU, REALLY?

ConsenSys, a software company in the United States, was founded with the intention to transform the digital world, adopting a remote-friendly approach even before the pandemic and managing over nine hundred employees in different time zones. Offering blockchain-based technology solutions to developers, enterprises, and individual consumers, it was established in 2015 by one of the Ethereum network creators, Joseph Lubin. While remote work was great for the company's productivity, ConsenSys and Lubin soon encountered struggles they hadn't foreseen regarding their employees' mental health.

The main challenge was a lack of office support for employees who worked remotely. A company-wide study showed that those who had no face-to-face interaction with other team members experienced loneliness and felt disconnected from their teams and goals. Full-time remote team members also worked long hours and had developed a poor work-life balance; they worked whole days but gave themselves few breaks, and they felt like they had little to no control. What had initially seemed to be a positive change—the ability to work from anywhere—quickly became a struggle to keep up with tasks.

As ConsenSys investigated the problem, it became clear that time zones and workflows were the culprits. Projects felt uncoordinated to employees and workflows were out of sync. ConsenSys leaders were particularly alarmed when a company-wide study showed that a majority of remote workers were facing burnout. Whereas many companies might have immediately rethought remote work in general, ConsenSys chose to address *how* it approached remote offices in order to ensure a more positive effect on the mental health and quality of life of those who worked from home. Remote work wasn't the problem; the company just hadn't taken the right steps to help its workers adapt to it.

The leaders chose an educative approach and introduced Remote-how Academy to the workplace, an external and online paid course with mentorship from leaders at companies like Buffer, Doist, and GitHub. The goal was to enable remote workers to adopt the right mindset toward their own and their coworkers' time, identify signs of burnout and reduce burnout, and refine their skills to be better remote workers. Employees enrolled in Remote-how Academy at the company's expense for four weeks.

The academy created a set of online courses to teach team members how to better perform in remote roles. Teams would go through these courses, with particular focus on the "self-care" module, and apply their learnings concurrently at work.

The ConsenSys managers were fully involved in the classes, using the lessons as an authentic and valuable learning experience to improve their global workflow. If successful, the classes could also serve as an onboarding system for new employees with no remote experience.

The pilot trial had many positive outcomes:

- Both leaders and team members learned new strategies to overcome loneliness.

- The program taught participants the importance of practicing self-care in a remote work environment.

- The program showed how better working habits would allow everyone to stay on top of their responsibilities.

- The effort made by ConsenSys showed its employees that the company cared and was invested in their future.

If you want to be a successful remote leader, you must pause and reflect on the mental health of your team members while also identifying ways to help overcome any obstacles associated with remote positions. Otherwise, leaders risk negating any of the benefits of remote work in the first place.

What can other companies learn from ConsenSys's experience? Prior to the pandemic, remote work was recognized as a flexible, beneficial, and rewarding "perk" favored among both management and employees. Leaders saw a cost-effective solution that allowed them to leverage talent and reduce staff turnover. Employees saw a chance to maintain a better work-life balance and have a more independent approach to their jobs—they engaged in remote work *voluntarily*. Generally, these remote positions were reserved for developers and other technical workers, creatives like writers or artists, and online customer service positions.

The uncertainty caused by the global health crisis changed the entire landscape of remote work. What was once voluntary and a perk is now standard. Positions, companies, and even industries that were never before a part of the remote-working world rushed to adapt to the new normal. Indeed, they had no choice, as offices were off-limits amid worldwide lockdowns. While many companies have admirably adapted to this new, globalized system of remote work, they now find themselves running into the same problems that ConsenSys once did. Workers are burning out faster and feeling more isolated than ever. For example, SAP SE, a SaaS (Software as a Service) company with a global headcount of over one hundred thousand, reported that more than 60 percent of its workers felt they were overworked, while a BambooHR survey reported that more than a third of respondents took a day off to reduce burnout last year.[1,2]

The reason behind this is simple: in an effort to quickly adopt a remote workforce, most managers and businesses did not put their workers' personal needs first, nor did they consider the mental ramifications of a global health crisis. As the office-based archetype is slowly vanishing, companies are trying to adapt through Zoom meetings, shared drives, online chats, and modern equipment.

But going remote comes with far more challenging issues such as isolation, poor mental health, and a general state of confusion. Often these issues are not discussed, bubbling under the surface, and most companies generally view them as less urgent than technical trouble-shooting. We need to address these changes holistically if companies are to adjust. While managers may successfully tick off their daily to-do list and increase company productivity, the actual challenges hide on a deeper level.

WHAT IS BURNOUT, AND WHY IS IT WORSE WHEN WORKING FROM HOME?

According to Mind Share Partners, a nonprofit focusing on workplace mental health, 42 percent of employees around the world have experienced deteriorating mental health since remote work became the norm in 2020.[3] In the same survey, 40 percent of respondents said that no one from their company asked whether or not they were doing okay, and 38 percent were more likely to agree that their mental health had worsened. It is thus important to consider how our relationship with work—which we all do for at least forty hours a week—has possibly worsened, and what this might mean for our overall mental health.

Burnout might feel like an overused term that appears in think pieces in the paper almost every day, but it cannot be ignored or glossed over if managers are to foster healthy relationships between their employees and the work environment. Recognized as a disease by the World Health Organization, burnout is a syndrome with symptoms like exhaustion, negativity, and reduced productivity, brought about by chronic stress. Indeed, a job aggregator found recently in a survey of 1,500 US workers that burnout is at an all-time high. Here are some more worrying statistics from the same survey:[4]

- Half of the responders experienced burnout in 2021, "up from the 43 percent who said the same in Indeed's pre-COVID-19 survey."

- In 2021, 59 percent of Millennial respondents said they were burned-out, up 6 percent from pre-pandemic burnout rates.

- Gen Z reported an increase in burnout from 47 percent to 58 percent between 2020 and 2021.

- Burnout among Baby Boomers, although still low at 31 percent, increased by 7 percent during the pandemic.

- Gen X saw burnout leap from 40 percent to 54 percent, the highest increase among generations.

It's hard to make generalizations about all remote-working environments from this one survey, but the fact that burnout is increasing across all generations is alarming. Merging work and life into the same place without warning has made adapting to remote work far more difficult than it would have been if it had been done both consciously and proactively.

One positive consequence is that for the first time a large swathe of the population is now working remotely, and we're able to see the pitfalls of virtual offices more clearly than ever before. This enables us to find solutions that can make remote work easier in the future. I believe these pitfalls or causes of burnout can be divided into four main categories: communication, isolation, energy, and self-esteem.

As discussed in previous chapters, digital communication cannot fully replace face-to-face interaction. A lack of synchronistic communication, especially for workers who are used to working in offices, is a hard thing to get used to. Emojis, phone calls, and constant chat messages hardly make up for the emotion and authenticity that is carried in even a simple watercooler conversation, and leaders need to be aware of the constant need for addressing this lack in their teams.

Remote work also comes with a heavy dose of isolation. While this may be favorable for some introverts and highly independent workers who enjoy their newfound freedom, it may not benefit your team as a whole. Today, people can spend hours in a room with only a computer and mobile phone screen for company. Poor communication and isolation can combine to erode trust between team members as discussed in chapter two, and it can also lead to overwork. Because employees are no longer in an office and aren't in sight of their coworkers, they don't really have a gauge of how much work anyone else is doing. This can make them feel anxious, leading to overwork.

For workers who live with family at home, isolation isn't as much of a problem as energy, or a lack thereof. A worker who has a family to take care of is unlikely to be sitting in a chair all day. In particular, team members with young children have less time to themselves than ever before, having to complete work tasks while also cooking meals, cleaning up, and entertaining their children. This problem has become even more drastic since schools moved to virtual environments too, and will remain so until things go back to normal.

Poor self-esteem is a particularly overlooked aspect of working remotely. Many leaders do not understand how to adequately communicate with their own employees, and team members often have to guess at their managers' expectations of them in the absence of face-to-face meetings. Employees may start second-guessing themselves and their work when the only communication coming from their managers might be some terse feedback.

When these factors combine and reach a certain level of tension, burnout occurs. There is usually a catalyst that causes the actual feeling of burnout, like an impending deadline, an impossible workload, a poor interaction with a supervisor, or perhaps even tensions related to family and home. The causes, however, boil up over time, and the problem must be addressed at the very root. As a leader, the first step to being able to do so is identifying when your team members are struggling in the first place.

IDENTIFYING SIGNS OF POOR MENTAL HEALTH

Identifying signs of potential burnout or mental difficulties among employees can be challenging in a virtual workforce. When talking to a person in an office environment, leaders can often quickly spot a problem and pull the person aside for an open and honest discussion. New or different body language or habits, or even changes in the quality of someone's work, are some simple signs or symptoms of a deterioration in mental health.

In digital interactions, however, all we usually see is a person's face (and that's only if we're on a video call), which doesn't offer any real insight into their current mood. Further, many people are particularly good at putting on a good face during a short interaction or a meeting because they don't want to seem like they're not enjoying their work. As a leader, if you want to identify signs of poor mental health, you're going to have to look deeper.

Reduced Productivity

One of the first indicators that something is not going as expected is reduced productivity. Employees may fail to meet deadlines, be late to respond to messages, or act disengaged. As a leader, you need to remember that this might not mean that an employee does not care about their role or simply wishes to leave their job. When a person's mind is overwhelmed and exhausted, it's hard to stay focused, avoid errors, and put in adequate effort. Productivity drops as a person fights to complete even the simplest tasks.

In most cases, the employee facing these issues will need some level of support and guidance to get back on track. Showing empathy plays a crucial role in letting your team members know that you and your company not only appreciate their efforts but also care about their mental state. Instead of judging their poor performance or criticizing low levels of productivity, think about the actual causes behind these changes. Then be forward-looking and focus on the changes you can make to your workflow and methods to prevent similar incidents with your other team members in the future.

Longer Work Hours

Some employees tend to get buried in tasks when working remotely. Starting earlier in the morning or staying online after others have logged out may indicate that a person is struggling to stay on top of their work. Competitive workplaces may even encourage a culture of optics wherein individuals try to outcompete one another to "show off" that they're working a lot. The erasing of boundaries between work and home may also encourage employees to work longer than usual. Remember how remote employees replace the time they no longer need to commute? By working longer.

In an office, employees are often encouraged to go home once their shift is over. The appearance of the cleaners and the need to commute home are indicators that remind them about life outside their workplace. Leaders have to replace these small rituals even in entirely virtual environments. If you're using productivity-measuring software, make sure to look out for signs that employees may be spending too much time working. Encouraging employees to wrap up their day at a reasonable time and to maintain some kind of work-life balance is a step we must take at all times.

Looking Tired and Disconnected

Some of your team members may not admit that they're facing difficulties or are unable to cope, but their expressions, body language, and focus during work calls will be obvious indicators, and you have to try to identify these changes. This will be particularly hard to do if the only synchronous interactions you have with your team members are in multiperson meetings. Team members are unlikely to share or betray emotions if many people are present. If you really want to know how your team is doing, take the time to schedule one-on-one meetings where you and your team members can give deep and honest feedback to each other.

HOW TO CREATE A POSITIVE WORK ENVIRONMENT

Remote work is here to stay and the role of the business leader remains largely the same: online or offline, leaders need to ensure that each employee receives the right level of support to complete their tasks efficiently and correctly. In a remote-working environment, this means putting policies and practices in place to support the strain that remote work has on mental and physical health and to allow people to have the space and time to recover from burnout.

The basis of a healthy workplace is created by fostering an environment of empathy and support. I wish there were some rules or norms I could talk about that would help you do this, but there simply aren't. All it takes—and this is easier said than done—is being more sensitive toward the goals, desires, and problems of your employees; improving your ability to notice any changes in their behavior; and creating an atmosphere where your team members do the same for one another. This requires you to lead from the front and by example. Only when you have created an environment where there is meaningful communication, where goals are aligned, and where your employees feel like they can be honest about what they feel, can you begin to address workplace mental health at its core. Here are some ways to do so.

Bring Rituals Online

As discussed in chapter one, office workers have rituals to help them enter a working state of mind, whether it's a commute to work, a cup of coffee in the morning, or simply entering an environment distinct from their home. Now that the line between home and work has blurred, leaders must create new digital rituals to replace those that help anchor an employee's sense of belonging and workplace identity. One often-overlooked ritual is "signing off" at the office, in which an employee powers off their computer, packs their bag, and heads home. Team members should do the same "signing off" when their remote workday has come to an end, helping them move into a nonwork state of mind.

Provide Mental Health Days

One of the simplest practices for leaders to implement is to introduce mental health days, allowing their employees to take a day off with no questions asked. Employees who may not be coping well with the changes in their work environment, who may have a growing list of personal issues and tasks they've been unable to manage due to longer working hours, or who may simply be feeling spent due to always being at home would benefit greatly from having a day off to rest, recharge, and address some of their personal, non-work-related chores. Giving your employees a voluntary day off reduces the likelihood of burnout and demonstrates care for their mental well-being.

Offer Mental Health Resources

Consider investing in your employees' mental health by adopting and curating resources targeted to their needs. Employee assistance programs are a great way to ensure that every staff member can confidentially discuss their problems, their worries, or any factors that may affect their performance. Like ConsenSys, you can also introduce educational programs that help your team members help themselves. Video counseling sessions, virtual classes, or mental health apps are also great resources that can help team members cope. And, of course, small, simple gestures and acts of kindness toward coworkers go a long way: treat team members to a meal voucher or an online gift card to show appreciation for their efforts.

Give Meaningful and Empathetic Feedback

Your team members should always feel comfortable turning to leaders when they come across any difficulty in their remote work. Try to schedule one-on-one video sessions to check in with your team members as often as possible. This will help build long-lasting relationships and trust, as well as allow you to identify any signs of troubles that may indicate that a person is struggling. By letting direct reports know that individual sessions are available to communicate and exchange insights about tasks, progress, and potential issues in their daily schedule, you will build mutual trust with your team members. You will then be able to work with them to find solutions to whatever has been holding them back.

Promote Self-Care

Self-care routines are often associated with physical wellness and fitness, but they're also important to our mental and emotional health. If you want your employees to practice self-care, you have to lead by example. Show them how you maintain your own work-life balance and the things you do to center yourself, let off steam, and manage your workload when it seems too heavy. Simultaneously, you have to ensure that you're giving your team members manageable workloads. If they have no time to practice self-care, then they are likely to feel even more stressed about having to fit something new into their routine.

Encourage Exercise and a Healthy Lifestyle

Don't underestimate the importance of exercise and physical well-being in maintaining a healthy mind. Working from home means less movement for everyone—no walks, no commutes, no running around the office to talk to different departments, no meetings with clients and coworkers, and potentially fewer hours for exercise as the workday gets longer. Exercise releases endorphins, which contribute to a happier, stronger, and more focused mind. It's also a great way to get people out the door and away from their screens and to help them take some time off from work, even if just for an hour. As a leader, you should always ensure that your employees have access to resources that help them stay on top of their physical health, and you should actively encourage them to exercise, even when they're physically isolated from one another.

Take Care of Yourself

If you're a leader making the transition from an office to a virtual environment, you've probably also noticed that there are now new roles you have to play. In addition to your regular tasks, you now have the added responsibility of making sure that your teammates are surviving and thriving, and that you, your company, and your team can all support one another. While taking on all these novel responsibilities, don't forget to care for your own mental health! Develop a mental health program for yourself that can also be a model for others by finding your own centering activities like exercise or journaling or speaking to a mental health professional if you're feeling low.

TAKAKO'S METHODS

Managing the world of remote work may seem challenging, but over time I've learned tricks to keep every member of my team looked after and happy in their individual roles. Remember that being a remote leader is no different from being an in-person leader—you're just as responsible for your employees' success. There are many activities that can help bring coworkers together while improving their mental and physical health. Here are some of my methods:

- Consider a mental health "pulse oximeter"—an anonymous survey sent out monthly to all employees asking them to indicate how they would rate their current state of mental health. Have someone oversee this initiative and dashboard, and then share insights with the wider community. Being honest about these feelings can help encourage trust and solidarity in the office.

- Ask, "How are you, really?" This sounds simple, but it really does work. It can help you pave the way for an honest conversation about how someone is doing in their home life as well as their work life and encourage you to think of solutions to their problems.

- Secure subscriptions to online exercises and wellness classes to boost activity and encourage staff members to stay active. You might provide a fitness budget whereby employees can be reimbursed for some dollar amount each month for physical or mental health expenses, such as a meditation app subscription.

- Encourage team members to communicate and make informal connections when managers and other leaders are not present. This might mean an informal metric that tracks the number of organic, one-on-one digital meetings between employees.

- Establish one-on-one check-ins between manager and employees where the only rule is to talk about anything that's not work related. This will help recreate casual chats and small talk that would naturally occur in an office environment.

- Encourage flexibility and emphasize the importance of taking breaks. Try creating a system in which workers are encouraged to sign off early if they have no work left for the day and to not bother those who have already signed off. Emails sent to those who have already signed off can have the words "[NOT URGENT]" in the header.

- Propose Friday lunch meetups where all employees can take their lunch break at the same time and have an online group lunch.

- Encourage socialization among peers. Suggest that staff members organize birthday surprises online and allocate time to celebrate one another's achievements (promotions, new babies, anything that would be celebrated in the real office environment).

- Lead by example and take mental health days when needed to encourage team members to come clean when facing difficulties.

- Build a virtual office culture to help employees feel supported. For example, create an office playlist for everyone to listen to, or organize casual meetings to catch up on non-work-related matters.

CHAPTER 6

THE MEETING

THE MEETING AS THE NEW OFFICE ENVIRONMENT

Running remote meetings successfully is challenging. Arranging them can be unwieldy, there are almost always technical issues, and the absence of a certain "human factor" can make them bothersome to sit through. Verdant Management, a management consultancy based in Australia, recognized that companies were facing real trouble adapting their meetings to the new, remote norm during the pandemic and began creating protocols to address their issues. Recently, it was asked to help one of its clients organize an annual general meeting (AGM) over video, bringing all of that company's stakeholders together in a "meeting room" via online videoconferencing channels.

The client, which had stakeholders across Australia and New Zealand, had been forced to cancel its face-to-face AGM due to the rise of COVID-19 cases in its region. The meeting required a 10 percent attendance rate of all members to make quorum, and a 75 percent majority vote to pass a special resolution that was in question. As such, it was essential that all video connections worked properly, that all members were able to attend with their home equipment, and that all of them were able to communicate quickly and efficiently. The meeting also had to be interactive enough to sustain attention and keep participants involved, and it was imperative to ensure that all the content set out for the annual meeting was easily accessible and presented in a manner appropriate for all stakeholders.

Verdant recommended Zoom to its client as the virtual meeting platform, given that it was being widely adopted at the time. In order to bring the spirit of the client's brand online, Verdant created a branded landing page that included a list of attendees and polls to gauge the interest of attendees in several different topics of discussion. The main challenge was ensuring that content was not only delivered in line with the meeting requirements, but also engaging. To address this, Verdant suggested that the information be presented as succinctly as possible and it reduced the main presentation from sixty-two slides to merely fifteen.

During the meeting, microphone access was given to all attendees when requested, and each was given the chance to speak if they wanted to. In addition, the attendees could use the Q&A feature to ask questions and could provide their feedback through the featured chatting system.

Because Verdant and its client planned carefully and ensured that real-life meeting roles were properly translated for a digital environment, the remote meeting resulted in a higher attendance rate than previous, in-person AGMs. The much shorter presentation time allowed for more interaction, and the ability to be included in verbal conversation with the executives kept other members more engaged and involved. Moreover, chatting and messaging functions also ensured that everyone was able to participate and quickly resolve any outstanding matters or concerns. During the in-person meetings, most members had kept quiet, but since questions over chat require less effort and less extroversion to be made and answered, more people expressed themselves.

Videoconferencing tools such as Zoom are of great benefit to businesses when used appropriately and can reduce the bloat and inefficiencies of in-person meetings. The challenge with video meetings, however, is fighting the isolation created by virtual environments. By using meetings that are carefully planned and designed to encourage members to talk and interact, leaders can build and maintain an online meeting culture and create new rituals, both of which are vital to building trust between team members and transitioning smoothly from an in-person to a virtual office environment.

By some estimates, an average organization spends close to 15 percent of its aggregate working hours in meetings, and midlevel managers spend more than a third of their time in meetings.[1] The more senior you become, the more meetings you end up sitting in! Chances are that as a leader, you've had to attend several meetings that you *knew* would be a waste of time beforehand, but you had no choice but to be there. For better or for worse, the reality is that meetings are a dedicated time and space for teams to align and connect with one another, and even in the absence of physical proximity, they are essential and are here to stay.

While remote working by its very definition is the end of the physical office environment, it doesn't necessarily do away with the core concepts of the office. Leaders need to make sure that the new meeting room—built around videoconferencing software—will empower and enable communication for teams rather than hamper them. This chapter will address how to have an effective meeting.

HAVE MEETINGS CHANGED?

Meetings in a virtual environment are supposed to serve the same purposes as those you have in an office: you and your team analyze past performance, iron out issues, and align on future goals. None of these purposes have materially changed for remote leaders. All the same, meetings seem to take up far more time and importance in remote work than they did in the office. According to the National Bureau of Economic Research, the aggregate number of business meetings has gone up by about 13 percent since the pandemic.[2] Why might this be the case?

The answer—and we've discussed this already—is communication and how it changes when we transition to a remote environment. Even though the forms of communication are greater in number than ever before, we still cannot replace the immediate in-person interactions of the office. You can no longer lean over your cubicle or step into your supervisor's office for a quick chat or discussion. Now you have to draft an email or instant message or, worse yet, schedule a virtual call just to grab some time with somebody. Consciously or unconsciously, we are now choosing to save these smaller, unplanned interactions that happened easily in the office for when we actually speak to one another; that is, we are choosing to make *everything* a meeting. This means losing out on a lot more time that can be better spent doing more important tasks.

There are other problems with virtual meetings too. It's far easier to drop off from a virtual meeting, muting yourself or turning off your camera to begin working on something else. Because you are not in a room filled with other, *real* people, or are not in an environment conducive to focus (especially if you're at home), you are far less likely to be engaged in the meeting itself and may lose out on learning important details or, worse yet, completely not notice when someone addresses you. Poor meetings mean poor communication, and poor communication means a less productive office and also potentially lower morale—sitting through dreary meetings day after day can really get to me, and I know it gets to you too.

So, meetings are more frequent than ever before, but they aren't going to get better unless we're proactive about addressing them. Doing so involves solving the problems of virtual meetings that I've mentioned above while also making the best use of new software and technology so that meetings can be more effective than ever before.

WHEN *NOT* TO HAVE A MEETING

The first step to having better meetings is knowing when *not to have one*. As leaders, we've all sat through meetings that we knew didn't have to happen, and this problem has only been exacerbated since most of the world has gone remote. Here are some examples of meetings that shouldn't occur:

- **Status updates:** If the only purpose of your meeting is to update and be updated on progress on tasks or projects, you should probably rethink having it. New applications and virtual collaboration tools make it incredibly easy to keep track of projects with team members—even in real time when using tools like Google Docs or Sheets—and you can use messaging features to ask questions, point out errors, or make edits. Morning stand-ups are a great way to get status updates out of the way quickly. We'll discuss them later on in the chapter.

- **Meetings with no visuals needed:** If your meeting does not need any visuals or you do not explicitly feel the need to see the faces (and reactions) of your team members, then a full virtual meeting may not be necessary. See the section below on using audio instead of video calls for more on this.

- **Meetings with no agenda:** If your meeting has no agenda beforehand, if no information is sent out on the meeting itself, and if your team members are not prepared for it, then it's likely to be a very ineffective form of communication. I have strict rules for pre-meeting requirements, which I'll also discuss further below.

BEST PRACTICES FOR CONDUCTING A REMOTE MEETING

Audio Versus Video

When I think about work from home, the first image that comes to mind is a computer screen filled with rectangles containing little heads and shoulders. In reality, however, getting people on video isn't necessary every time a meeting is held. I usually require cameras when

I'm hosting a large meeting, because I like to see the reactions of my coworkers to certain proposals or ideas. In fact, this is one of the advantages of using videoconferencing for meetings—it's hard to see the reactions of *everyone* in an office meeting, but it's far easier to do this on a small screen.

In large meetings, I also usually find myself needing visuals, in the form of either presentations or a screen someone is sharing with the rest of the team. In these cases, video calls are necessary.

For one-on-one or large meetings where you do not need to reference any digital materials or emails, I strongly recommend voice calls. On calls, we tend to pay more attention to the voice and content of what a person is saying, instead of worrying about our physical appearance and how we look to the other participants. Have you ever noticed that you, or perhaps your coworkers or supervisor, gesture instinctively on phone calls? This is a sign of being deeply engaged in a discussion. But have you ever caught yourself gesturing in a video call and then felt a little more self-conscious about your posture and the positions of your hands in front of your computer? It happens to me all the time.

Audio-only calls are also more appropriate for harder conversations about sensitive topics, such as a difficult decision you have to make or perhaps even a personal issue that needs to be discussed with a team member. Calls help get to the heart of the problem by negating the need to have to physically present yourself in a work-appropriate manner. A colleague once gave me the following advice: "If you ever feel like someone you're close to needs to tell you something but can't get it out of themselves, take them on a drive and see if that helps them loosen their tongues a little." When you're not looking at each other, it becomes far easier to focus on words and their meaning. The same logic applies to an audio-only call, which might provide the kind of space that video calling lacks.

Once you've figured out which situations are most appropriate for audio and video calls, set the rules down in a document and share it with all your team members. Ensure that the guidelines are followed for subsequent meetings.

Scheduling Meetings

As a leader, you should always know what, exactly, a meeting is for. If you don't, cancel it. This might seem a little harsh, but this is the rule that I've set for myself, and I've also made the rule very clear to my fellow coworkers and team members so that there are no exceptions.

When I send out a meeting invite, I like to write *at least* three bullet points about what I'd like to cover in the meeting, to help guide the meeting and allow team members to prepare for specific discussions. These invites also occasionally have a shared document attached in which teammates can provide input on what they would like to discuss and how much time they think they will need for each topic.

I'm also a big proponent of short meetings; most of those I schedule are either twenty or forty-five minutes long. Shorter meetings tend to make team members far more aware of how much time they have to discuss topics, encourage discussions that are to the point, avoid bloat and small talk, and make presentations more succinct.

With regard to actual timing, always send out a meeting invite at least twenty-four hours in advance to give yourself and others time to prepare. Make sure to choose a time that is reasonable for all your team members (neither too early nor too late), and if you run an international office, make sure to keep a list of time zones handy to avoid mishaps—2 PM in New York is 3 AM in Tokyo! I've been there, take my word for it.

Meeting Prep

Creating a pre-meeting checklist is key to making sure your meetings are consistently successful. Here are a few tips I use:

- **Software:** Make sure to have all the software you need for a meeting with your team, and ensure that you have backup conferencing tools in case your main medium fails for any reason. At our office, we use Zoom and Google Meet. If you're having meetings with clients, customers, or other business partners, make sure to be on the same page about which software you're going to use. As an international business leader, I have many clients who live in countries where certain kinds of software are restricted, so I always make sure to know what platform we will be using well before the meeting.

- **Meeting materials:** Make sure to have all your notes, presentations, and other documents prepared before the meeting. I like to print my material and have it in my hand, if possible, in addition to opening and arranging all the relevant windows on my computer screen so I don't have to fumble around during a meeting. Review these documents and look to see if your team members have sent anything new.

- **Time check:** As I've said above, make sure to time your meeting right, *double-checking* that you're looking at the correct time zone.

- **Personal appearance:** If you're on a video call, make sure you are dressed appropriately. I'm a big believer in the mantra "look good, feel good," and as such, I try to dress for a virtual meeting as I would for one in person. Right before I join the actual meeting, I also do a quick check on my local webcam to make sure everything is in place and I don't have any ungainly stains on my clothing or any food between my teeth.

- **Webcam:** Buy a laptop stand or stack some books underneath your laptop to raise your camera to your eye level. This will help you feel like you are talking more directly to your meeting attendees.

- **Virtual backgrounds:** As far as possible, clean up the background behind you and feel free to leave in books or other objects that convey your personality. Whatever you choose, be prepared and willing to talk about it, as small talk may end up centering around observations from your meeting attendees. While many types of meeting software have background blur and green screens, I would not recommend them, as they make things less personal and can sometimes be quite distasteful or distracting.

During the Meeting

If you're having a meeting with more than five people, I always recommend using an administrative cohost. You can give this duty to one of your team members at the beginning of the meeting or assign it beforehand. The cohost's role will be to mute those who forget to mute themselves, unmute coworkers who would like to speak, monitor the chat for questions or concerns, and point out anything that you, the leader, might have missed. This ensures that the less self-aware or less tech-savvy participants do not disrupt the flow of the meeting and that you can focus on the meeting and its content instead of being distracted by petty details. If you would like to record the meeting, inform the cohost beforehand.

I always begin my meetings by laying out the meeting rules. In addition to getting everyone on the same page, it's also a good way to help everyone transition to the meeting mindset. If you're recording the meeting, make sure to let everyone know at this point. Remind everyone who the cohost is and that you expect them to turn on their cameras (if the meeting requires it), to mute themselves when they're not speaking, and to press the Raise Hand function if they have anything urgent to say; finally, state how long the meeting is going to run. Also have your cohost post the rules in the chat area. After all, you are leading the meeting and have every right to run it the way you'd like.

These are all general rules, but as a leader you may also have your own, special rules. A colleague I work with has all her team members close out of their inboxes and browsers and turn their phones upside down. While attending her meetings feels a little bit like being in a college classroom, they're particularly efficient. She commands everyone's attention because of this simple request, and there is an energy of active participation for the full ninety minutes.

If you're having a smaller meeting where some of the participants do not know one another, take a moment for brief introductions before you lay out the rules. Just as you would introduce two strangers to each other if they met in person, so should you strive to give people the chance to meet each other over Zoom. I can't recall how many times I've had to stop meetings from starting right away, because not everyone on the Zoom call knew one another. By connecting others, you connect disparate dots in your organization, which allows more room for the cross-pollination of ideas and solutions.

Once your meeting is underway, try to create engagement rather than having people drone on and on individually. Answer any questions that may pop up in the chat, ask both senior and junior team members for their opinions, and try to include as many of your colleagues in the discussion as is both possible and reasonable. In large meetings, this may sometimes feel like cold-calling people, which may be a little harsh but is necessary if you want to make sure everyone is paying attention.

During a virtual meeting, it's particularly important for leaders to maintain energy levels. I've found that orchestrating and running a video or audio call takes more energy and effort than it would in person. People are naturally more inclined to be passive and introverted and to sink into their chairs while staring at a screen; it's a visceral reaction and it's natural when you're not sitting next to people in a physical environment. Unfortunately, there aren't too many tricks to holding participants' attention. In addition to occasionally engaging team members in the discussion and presenting material as succinctly as possible, providing microbreaks can help your team maintain their focus. These are short one- or two-minute breaks where members can stretch their legs, blink their eyes hard a few times, and refill their coffee. Needless to say, if you're having a longer meeting that stretches for hours, please give your team members longer breaks.

If your team meeting is an internal one, you have a little more room in terms of what you can do with these breaks. You can use them to discuss the news, talk about sports scores, or have a little stand-up session. The point here is to mix things up and to make meetings unpredictable, which can introduce an element of surprise and excitement for coworkers who might be too passive or easily distracted in your meetings.

Always stick to the agenda and the times that you have set for the meeting. If you allow the discussion to wander into irrelevant or unrelated areas, you risk having the meeting become unwieldy and might not fulfill the original goals you had for the meeting. I'm a stickler for timing. When topics or whole meetings have been assigned a certain amount of time, either my cohost or I make sure that we don't go over the limit. This might seem like it restricts discussion or prevents spontaneity, but if you set the expectations in the agenda and in your instructions prior to the actual meeting, then this rule is not that hard to follow. And in time, if you practice this discipline regularly, you will find that your team learns to regulate itself and that your meetings are far more efficient and fruitful.

Wrapping Up the Meeting

As you wind down the meeting, save some time to resolve any concerns or questions that attendees may have. Addressing problems as they arise will help avoid any future confusion or miscommunication. After the meeting, if you need to have other meetings in the future, it also helps to create a schedule for everyone on subsequent meetings and outline the expectations and goals for those meetings, as well as a rough agenda. Make sure to disseminate any materials from the meeting. This can include an audio recording, presentations from the meeting, and documents produced during the meeting itself.

Once you are alone, ask yourself if the meeting was necessary or a waste of time. Did the meeting cover all the topics you had set on the agenda? If the meeting was not as productive as planned, analyze what went wrong by going through the agenda, looking at what the meeting produced, and asking other attendees for their feedback.

You can also ask team members to meet without you and to propose what they think is the best meeting cadence and style of meeting. The key thing that you, as a leader, must do is to assure them that your schedule is flexible and that you trust their judgment. I once was able to do this with my group at my former employer, Procter & Gamble, and I found that employees felt more empowered and made the meeting "theirs," looping me in and using me to help where I could instead of expecting me to take the lead. This meant I actually had to attend fewer meetings, because my team members could meet on their own to take care of minor tasks—the dream of every remote leader!

TAKAKO'S METHODS

I use a variety of alternatives to the traditional meeting, which go beyond the standard half-hour or hours-long Zoom or Teams sessions. If meetings have a predefined purpose, they can be anything a leader wants them to be. They can be a place of spontaneity where team members brainstorm together, learn together, and build together. Team members can even work online together, as if they were in the same team room; in such situations, close proximity and a live channel between team members can actually help them complete many of their tasks and solve communication problems.

Here are some alternatives to the same old drab virtual meetings:

- **Quick stand-ups**: While I've discussed this earlier, I cannot help reiterating how important they are in a virtual context.

A stand-up is exactly what it sounds like. All attendees must stand up and have a quick round-robin meeting where each person reports on what they're working on for the day or week, the issues or problems that they're working through, and any other updates that the other team members need to know. The goal is to have each teammate present a status update on their individual workstreams and to have the meeting be short enough so that everybody can feel comfortable standing the whole time (hence the name). Mine usually take five to thirty minutes (anything longer will require an actual meeting), and I usually have them in the morning. I've found stand-ups to be one of the most effective types of meetings, because everybody can get straight to the point of what has been done, what is being done, and what still needs to be done.

- **Online workshops:** We've all attended workshops. Moving them online is much easier than you might think. The point of a workshop is to have everyone learn together, and with software today like Google Jamboard, there are numerous ways to have someone lead a collaborative learning session in a fun and visually engaging way. Workshops help spice things up once in a while and offer a chance for you, as a leader, to off-load some duties to other teammates who can share their insights or learning and lead a conversation. For example, in my roles I've always organized a weekly learning session, where anyone who attends must come and share something that they learned that week or month. It's a knowledge-sharing workshop where people can add their observations about others' insights. I find that workshops are the kind of meetings most likely to spark innovation in my teams.

- **Informal meetings:** Some of my most useful meetings are informal sessions, where there is no agenda and anyone can come to the meeting to speak their mind about matters both inside and outside work. The inspiration comes from traditional Quaker meetings, where people take turns sharing their thoughts on topics that matter to them. In this case, attendees choose the agenda, and the meeting can be a place to blow off steam and build community among team members.

- **Online brainstorming sessions:** In these sessions, the sole goal is divergent thinking. The team chooses one topic, and everybody tries to list out ideas without fear of judgment. These sessions are usually rapid-fire to ensure that people don't have to think too hard and filter themselves, and team members contribute one after another in quick succession. Brainstorming always includes a visual element, and I use a virtual whiteboard so we can visualize our ideas in real time.

- **Online coworking sessions:** The coworking session is the anti-meeting. Here, remote team members voluntarily log on to a "meeting" where they can work alongside their coworkers. The idea is to replicate the feeling of the office. There is no set agenda and you're not discussing specific topics, but you're each working on your specific tasks and can occasionally turn on your audio or video to have a quick informal chat, ask questions, or discuss a problem.

CHAPTER 7

ON MINIMIZING DISTRACTIONS

FOCUS, FOCUS, FOCUS

Around summer 2021, companies across the world prepared to welcome workers back to their offices. For many of these organizations, the pandemic and remote working had brought about a rethink on the purposes of the office and what the ideal office should look like. Gone are the days when open offices were the norm; floor space is being reduced as fewer workers are needed at the office full-time; and many companies are even reconsidering what kind of furniture they want in their offices.

Of the companies concerned about the latter, Spotify is the most prominent. In addition to reimagining its floor plans, the company is also introducing a kind of focus "pod," produced by the Estonian company Silen, into its offices. On its website, Silen describes its products as "unique modular silent spaces"[1] and states that "each pod has an air circulation system, splashproof electrical sockets, and automatically controlled LED lights."[2] The pods are also modular and can be connected to one another.

A glance through Silen's website will show you futuristic-looking (and perhaps even dystopian) phone booths where workers can sit and get their task done in a kind of bubble, separated from the rest of the office. Silen seems to be blowing up after the pandemic, as companies rethink how staff gets work done—there are now pods in the offices of Amazon, Volkswagen, and Coca-Cola, among others.

It's almost as if the pandemic has led to a reconsideration of focus or, more accurately, just how hard it is to really focus. Working from home includes a bevy of distractions both digital and otherwise. It's not just notifications but also children, pets, partners, doormen, packages, poor internet connection . . . the list goes on and on.

Yet many people won't be going back to an office now, hybrid or otherwise. And buying a Silen pod for the home isn't a feasible option either—they run into tens of thousands of dollars each and actually take up quite a lot of space. If workers want to be able to focus in their home, they have to learn how to create their own pods through discipline, rituals, and planning.

Reorienting your focus is in many ways a personal project. There is only so much you can do to encourage others to focus, beyond creating an environment that is conducive to doing so. It requires dedication, effort, and a well-thought-out plan. If you, as a leader, want to spread the best focus practices in your virtual office, you must lead by example and show others how you create a space for yourself that is conducive to efficiency and productivity. This chapter thus addresses what you, the leader, can do to increase your own focus, rather than telling you how to lead your team members. Read on to learn how you can optimize your home or other non-office workspace for maximum focus and efficiency.

IDENTIFYING NEW DISTRACTIONS

When I worked in an office, my brain naturally adjusted to "work mode." The surroundings, the clothes, the rituals, the colleagues: all of these reminded me I was no longer at home. That's not as easy to do from home, and there are also *new* challenges that prevent us from focusing. Home environments aren't conducive for work unless we actively make them so; there are too many factors and disturbances that lie beyond our control.

Additionally, procrastination has taken on new forms for many of us this past year. We are humans that crave social experiences. Lacking these, we seek them online, and this naturally turns us to the convenient distractions that the web offers, from social media to news to LinkedIn (which I've been guilty of mindlessly browsing like it's Instagram).

Focusing is generally harder today because we live in the attention economy. Every company is competing not just for your money and wallet but also for your time and attention. Three seconds of your attention on an ad, a scroll from top to bottom of a web page, or a few more click-throughs on a website: these are all ways you help companies monetize their products, by boosting metrics that lead to higher revenue. Remember, if the product is free, then your attention is the cost.

A lack of focus can be very stressful. It makes it harder to work and complete tasks, making you feel like you're falling behind and not achieving your true potential. This can create a vicious cycle where we seek out more distractions to keep from facing tasks at work, falling even further behind. Given these new challenges to our ability to focus, it's now more important than ever to be disciplined in choosing where we direct our attention.

The root causes for our perpetual state of distraction today are many: our environment, our mindset, our tendency to procrastinate, and more—all of which we should reflect on, accept, and seek to change.

SETTING UP THE ENVIRONMENT TO PREVENT DISTRACTIONS

We each need a dedicated workspace optimized for productivity. To create this, you must first carve out a designated area just for you in your home. If you don't have your own room, then claim a dedicated table and shelf for all your work needs. Speak with your partner, family, or housemate to ensure their stuff doesn't sprawl into your area, and likewise make sure to be respectful of their designated space too.

Everything in and around your workspace should help you focus. The first step to achieving this is outfitting your area with a setup—a table, a chair, and computer equipment—that is comfortable for you and streamlines your work. If you're sitting (or standing) more than a few hours a day, then you need to make sure you are treating your body in the best way possible. If your body feels at ease, so will your mind, and you will complete tasks with ease.

Posture is nature's free gift to you, and poor posture is often overlooked when thinking about your body and its relation to work. Good posture increases the amount of oxygen that reaches your brain. It makes you less prone to long-term injuries to your spine and back, and it reduces neck and other alignment issues. Good posture can also make you more aware and mindful and creates a kind of harmony between your mind and body. You wouldn't slouch in a big meeting or while giving a talk, so why slouch at home alone?

To help you with posture, the first thing to evaluate in your workspace is the chair on which you sit for most of your workday. You sit on your chair for far longer than you lie on your bed (unless you work from your bed, which I absolutely do not recommend if you can avoid it). Chairs are universal objects that we take for granted, and you might think that you can just substitute an Ikea dining chair for your office chair. This is far from the truth—you'll immediately notice the difference when you try out an office chair that helps support your back.

There's a reason that Scandinavian furniture, especially chairs, is renowned for its design: it evolved with the functionalism movement. The designers actually looked at how people sit in chairs, measured their limbs and hips, and examined how their feet rest on the ground. They then tailored the height, contours, and angles of all their furniture to match their empirical studies.

This is all to say, go and find a chair that fits you and your body. Given that remote work will be around in some form for the rest of our lifetimes, I'd go so far as to say that it's wise to invest in a high-quality chair such as a Herman Miller or Steelcase. Wouldn't you be willing to spend more on a nicer mattress if it meant better sleep? Even Ikea makes some ergonomic chairs today.

Regarding tables, their surface should be high enough to allow you to work on your computer without slouching over, and your elbows shouldn't feel strained when your hands are elevated on the table.

Personally, I'm partial to standing while at work, and I use a kind of stand that elevates my laptop to the ideal height.

Another thing to consider is your monitor height. During meetings, it's easy to tell who is hunched over their computer's webcam with bad posture and who looks like they're sitting straight-backed as if they're in a real meeting room. Here's a tip: get a dedicated home monitor, or get a laptop stand, a mouse, and a keyboard. You can clamp your monitor onto your table for easy elevation and adjust it so that the middle of the screen sits right at the level of your eyes. You will find yourself with your chin higher and your neck in a better position. You will be look-ing straight at the camera and your screen, with your meeting attendees seeing your beautiful frontal profile instead of a bottom-up view of your nostrils. You will, incidentally, appear more confident as well.

Finally, if you have the opportunity, ask your company or manager if they can provide a work-from-home budget for employees to buy these efficiency-enhancing workplace items. After all, your company is paying much less in office maintenance costs, so its leaders would be wise to invest those savings in their employees' at-home productivity. If you're in a position to make this happen at your office, I would highly recommend discussing it with HR or other decision makers.

MINIMIZING DISTRACTIONS THROUGHOUT THE DAY

There are three kinds of distractions, all of which are inevitable and a natural part of our lives.

The first type of distraction is one that directly interrupts your attention, like the unexpected arrival of a package or a disruption by your pet, housemate, or child. You may have seen the famous 2017 video clip of a BBC reporter interrupted by his two children while streaming live from his home office, before his wife drags them out of the room. The clip is both adorable and hilarious, but I can imagine that it did not feel that way for him at the moment.

A simple lesson to be learned from that clip is to set some rules for your housemates, and this includes your pets! For family members or roommates, you might send a simple text message expressing your need to hunker down for a few hours and asking them not to reach out to you unless it's an emergency. For children, you have to be extremely clear about your needs. One creative solution might involve crafting a "Do not disturb" sign to be hung on the door.

The second kind of distraction is one that creeps up on you and nags at you all day. This is a non-work-related distraction that demands your attention because you're not at the office or not in an environment that can help hide such distractions from you. This kind of distraction can range from having too many notifications on your phone to having to deal with tasks at home. For me, the most glaring distractions are in fact chores, like dishes that need to be done, clothes that need to be folded, and groceries that need to be managed. These are the necessities of day-to-day living that build up and become a distraction.

The final kind of distraction is one that we bring about by ourselves. We're fallible humans and are prone to procrastinating and distracting ourselves when we don't want to put in the effort to finish tasks or are having trouble completing tasks we do not enjoy.

Addressing these three kinds of distractions means creating an environment that is conducive to focus. While we will always have these distractions throughout the day, there are a few things we can do to minimize both their frequency and their impact:

- Ahead of the workday, change into office attire, even if you're staying at home. Not only will this wake you up, but seeing your crisp self will make you feel good, and when you feel good, you will perform better. Furthermore, wearing office clothing helps signify to you and your family members that you are in "working mode," not in "home mode." As a bonus, your family will also appreciate that you look sharp for your meals together!

- Leave your house for a walk or activity at least once in the morning and once in the afternoon or evening. The more this can become a ritual, the better. I've found that for many it's all too easy to find an excuse to stay home and work all day. You may feel that you're being more productive by staying home, but the truth is that you're more likely to be distracted if you don't take breaks or change your setting at some point during the day.

- Establish a dedicated time for reading the news in the morning before you start work. Don't jump straight into your email or team platform.

- Use time blocking to create time for chores. In those blocks, do nothing but focus on the chores at hand. This will allow you to get them done more quickly and not have them at the back of your mind for the rest of the day. Since I know I hate chores, I make sure to do them before I start work.

- Try deleting your work email app from your phone. This way, you will work only when you're in your workspace, creating a stronger association between "work mode" and your work area. Use your time away from your workspace to focus on nonwork things.

- Turn off all notifications and badges for your apps. Use your phone when you want to, not when it wants you.

FOCUSING BETTER DURING MEETINGS

It can be tough to focus during remote meetings, especially those that are not directly relevant to your work, or in which you won't need to be an active participant. You might even think, "This is useless and boring," or "Why am I here?" It wouldn't be socially acceptable to express these thoughts out loud, but it's natural and normal to feel this way. Remote meetings also make it very easy to multitask. It's easy to sit there with your camera and microphone off, sneakily working on another task that you think is more important than the meeting.

However, there are also ways to proactively prevent these kinds of distractions. The first step is to correct your attitude right before your meeting by resetting yourself to a kind of mental state that is conducive to discussions. I call this state the "zero mind." Think about it as the tare feature on a scale, by which you reset the mass to zero. In your case, you reset any negative or distracting impulses in your mind to zero.

To achieve a zero mind, I recommend doing a small meditation or reflection session before longer, bigger meetings or tasks. The point here is to reset your awareness and center it on the task at hand. You can sit on the floor or a chair for this exercise. For beginners who haven't dabbled with meditation, one way to do this is to focus on your breathing. A quick Google search will show you many different techniques to choose from, so you can pick the one that best suits you.

The one I choose to do looks a little bit like this: I close only one nostril with my fingers and then inhale, hold, and exhale for five seconds each. I then repeat the same with the other nostril, cycling through the exercise four or five times. This brings my attention back to the immediate present and lets me temporarily park my worries or other irrelevant tasks.

Over time, I've also developed an attitude during meetings that is conducive to focus. Even if I am the host of a meeting or the one who called it, I always enter the meeting with the knowledge that I will be learning something new or, more specifically, something new that I was not aware of at all. This might seem a little simple, but it's a particularly useful attitude to have because it serves two purposes: (1) you're open to learning new things, and (2) you're more likely to pay attention if you believe that the person speaking is going to tell you something you don't know already. As such, instead of being a passive attendee at a meeting, you can play an active role and make it relevant to *yourself*. If you're a note taker, write down "What don't I know?" at the top of your notepad as a kind of mantra to keep you focused.

I also enter every meeting with notes prepared beforehand, as well as at least three questions I need clarified by my colleagues. I might find that they answer my questions without my having to ask them, but that just means I was listening to what they were saying (that is, paying attention).

If you find yourself still having difficulties paying attention during meetings, one trick is to make yourself write a memo to yourself at the end of every meeting. This way, you ensure that you're at least making some attempt to recollect the key points discussed, and you can then share your memo with other participants so they can weigh in on whether or not they agree on your takeaways. The point of all these tricks is to gamify your meeting by giving yourself a task that helps you stay engaged.

I've had some colleagues ask me if it's okay to multitask during a meeting or (God forbid) try to attend two meetings at once. A personal pet peeve of mine is when people are visibly doing something else during a meeting. I believe that a meeting is an opportunity for everyone to speak their minds so the group can get some degree of alignment or identify differences of opinion. If you're not fully present, you're essentially telling others that your viewpoint doesn't matter. And if that's true, then your time would be better spent on another meeting or task.

USING A REAL SCHEDULE TO STAY ON TRACK

Over the years, I've developed a routine for remote work that has helped me get used to its ups and downs, but it hasn't always been a smooth ride. Like many remote workers today, I initially made the mistake of not making an actual schedule for myself. This lack of planning and organizing meant I often felt like I was chasing my own tail, spending over twelve hours in front of my screen while still failing to complete my to-do list.

Running through a workweek without a schedule often leads to failure. Being far away from your office and other team members can make planning and scheduling difficult, but they are important factors in staying productive. Planning the time that you need to complete your tasks, attend meetings, and even take breaks is as vital to your success as a remote-working leader as it was when you managed people in an office.

After many setbacks, I learned to change my approach and segmented my day as if I were working in an actual office. Instead of jumping straight from bed and running to my laptop, I started with a firm routine that began when I meditated in the morning and ended when I turned off my computer in the evening. The system that I follow today is called time blocking. It means allocating a block of time for each task or activity and no other, in order to stay organized and productive throughout the day.

Each person must figure out the structure that works best for their needs. For me, my mornings are usually divided into two blocks. The first block is focused on high-priority work, while more flexible tasks are left for the second. Each block lasts half an hour to three hours. One of the most important blocks in my day is my lunch break, which I use to divide my mornings from my afternoons. Afternoons are reserved for creative work and client meetings, divided into their own blocks, followed by a short break. The last block of my workday is focused on planning tomorrow's tasks and my workflow for the next few days.

The key to this block system is preventing blending between the blocks, as far as possible. This approach not only helps me focus and stay organized, but also minimizes any distractions. It helps me think more deeply as I work and enables me to complete my tasks faster. Tuning into a "deep work" phase or working in absence of any distraction is not a skill that everyone can master at first—but practicing and turning it into a habit will pay off.

There is another alternative to the block system. You probably have a good sense of the tasks you have to finish on any given day. You might view them as emails in your inbox or on to-do lists that you've stored in your laptop or mobile phone so that you don't forget. I want to challenge you to take on a different method and mindset toward your tasks.

Begin your day with a pen and paper and write down the to-dos that you remember in order of urgency. They don't all have to be work related; you can even include house chores that you want to finish before, during, or after work. The goal is to think broadly and to identify all the tasks that you could feasibly finish that day. By writing your to-dos down rather than relying on software, you not only prioritize the tasks that you really want to finish, but also become more committed to them and more likely to actually complete them.

In a similar vein, I try to do a high-level thinking exercise at the beginning of each week in which I write down between one and three big projects (or components of a project) that I need to finish that week. While using software and virtual collaboration tools on your computer will help you complete these tasks, I find that forced self-reflection through the use of analog tools helps me reorient my focus and accomplish my actual priorities.

Encouraging yourself and your team members to practice blocking and deep-work modes will help not only establish rituals but also set work boundaries, allowing you and your team to clearly identify when the workday ends and letting everyone wind down and disconnect for the day.

AN UNDERRATED SKILL: KNOWING WHEN TO STOP

Sometimes poor focus isn't caused by distractions or interruptions or poor planning. You may just be feeling out of it, approaching burnout, and feeling fatigued. If you're unable to focus consistently, it's important to recognize that there is in fact a time to *stop* working on something for the day or afternoon—and I believe that knowing when to stop is an incredibly underrated skill.

When I worked in an office, I found myself focusing on managing my time and balancing it among my various commitments. But now that I work at home, I find myself focusing on managing my energy. As we no longer have the divide between office and home, it can be incredibly draining to transition from leading back-to-back meetings to suddenly realizing you need to figure out something for lunch. Different tasks either deplete or replenish our energy, and the trick is realizing when your time and effort can be better spent on something else.

In such a situation, you can ask yourself, Am I reaching the point of diminishing returns? Will I be able to finish this task at hand with a burst of energy when I feel more rejuvenated, perhaps even tomorrow? It's important throughout the day to gauge your energy level for your work, which can be much harder to measure than your energy level for free-time activities. Just because you have the time to create another PowerPoint or Excel model doesn't mean your energy would be best spent on that task at that moment or would lead to the best result. Sometimes, it's okay to leave for tomorrow what you can do (poorly) today.

METHODS FOR HELPING YOUR TEAM FOCUS

As a leader, you may be able to buckle down and focus on just about any task thrown at you—but that doesn't necessarily mean the same for your team members. Working on their ability to focus is vital to your team's overall productivity. Many of the people you manage might be victims of their own habits, and showing them a way to alter old habits or develop new healthy habits for focusing can work wonders.

Rohto has an interesting policy that often raises some skepticism from my friends when I tell them about it. Employees are allowed to work on any nonwork project or second job, as long as it does not impede their normal job responsibilities. The idea behind the policy is that it encourages employees to think more about how they use their time, how they spend their energy, and what matters most to them. It's a little radical, but the practice works: it's helped improve productivity by about 70 percent and it's also allowed me to pursue a directorship at another company without having to give up any of my duties at Rohto.

The key lesson here is that you must get your team members to think deeper about their time and how they spend it. You can improve their focus by helping them gauge their own energy and attention levels. Encourage them, by example, to become more self-aware and to recognize when they're better off doing something else and coming back the next hour, or day, or even week, rejuvenated and ready to work.

TAKAKO'S METHODS

Here are a few tips for leaders who want to help their employees focus better:

- If your company can afford it, create an employee fund that will allow your team members to invest in equipment to create a dedicated workspace at home.

- Encourage your employees to practice some of the techniques we've discussed in this chapter. Lead by example and be honest with your employees about your own experiences in managing your focus while working at home.

- Provide your employees with the means to separate their work and home lives. Your team members must have the flexibility to turn off when they wish. Set some basic rules to make this clear. For example, you might establish that you will contact them after 6 PM only when a task is urgent.

- While not all companies will be comfortable following policies like Rohto's regarding second jobs, do encourage your team members to pursue projects on their own and even other interests if these fit into their schedules. This will help them think deeper about what they're spending their time on and what really matters to them.

- During team meetings, have everyone quickly report their energy level. This is one of my favorite team rituals because it can be fun hearing a range of answers. Some may report 100 percent, while others may report 10 percent. The point is for everyone to be honest here so that their expectations for one another's work are set appropriately.

- If it's crunch time for a select team of people working hard on a deadline, consider ordering lunch to their addresses so they won't have to worry about cooking. This not only saves them time but also can be a pleasant surprise.

CHAPTER 8

THE NEW LEADER

NAVIGATING VIRTUAL ROLES AND NOVEL RESPONSIBILITIES

There was an article in the *Financial Times* titled "US and Europe Split on Bringing Bankers Back to the Office" that caught my eye recently, not for its generalizations on the difference between European and American banking culture, but for what it taught me about the different kinds of leadership paths open to us in the world of remote work.[1]

The article talks about an apparent "transatlantic rift" between American and European bankers, in which the former want their employees to return to the office and face-to-face meetings (once the pandemic is under control with surety), while the latter see remote work as the future and don't mind if their employees continue to work from home, and also see remote or hybrid office-remote work as the future of all banking.

The voice of the American cohort is led by Jamie Dimon, chairman and CEO of JPMorgan Chase, who decries a culture of Zoom meetings, going so far as to say he's "done with it." Mr. Dimon wants to bring his workers back to the office, citing that "clients told him that in cases where JPMorgan lost business to peers, it was because 'bankers from the other guys visited, and [JPMorgan's] didn't.'" Other, unnamed supporters of returning to the office worry that remote work will negatively affect company culture, hinder them in keeping employees happy and well trained, and hamper their ability to be competitive.

Meanwhile, Europeans are represented in the article by the chief executives of their largest bank. Frédéric Oudéa, chief executive of French lender Société Générale (SocGen), dismisses Dimon's concerns and goes on to say that "the idea that winning is just about spending 22 hours during the day at the office" is outdated. He also announced that SocGen would allow its employees worldwide to work from home three days a week, also claiming that the policy would "give [SocGen] a recruitment advantage with 'young talents' who 'don't see the world in the same way they did just two years ago.'"

I don't have any comments here about any purported and innate differences between Americans and Europeans, but this article is useful for us because it tells about two potential paths for leadership in the postpandemic world. Dimon clearly sees the merits of physical presence and its associated qualities of personality and charisma. Without this, he doesn't even see his bank being able to function normally. He can be considered, in this context, the voice of the "old guard," leaders who want the world to go back to being what it once was.

Oudéa and his colleagues, however, seem to have noticed the changing tides. They recognize that presence is no longer as necessary to the functioning of their businesses, and—crucially—they also seem to pay heed to the desires of the incoming workforce, a whole generation of young workers who have never worked in an office and, as such, may not even see the appeal of one.

Oudéa's concerns are also backed up with data: a survey of one thousand American workers in the summer of 2021 found that as many as 39 percent would consider quitting their jobs if they weren't presented with flexible working options, with that proportion rising to 49 percent for Millennial and Gen Z workers.[2] This may also be why workers in the United States are recording all-time-high quitting rates from their jobs.[3] Why settle for less when your friends and colleagues aren't?

Many leaders are ready to use these changes to their advantage. As banks like JPMorgan and Citi push to get their workers back into the office as quickly as possible, UBS and Lazard are offering juicy incentives: join and you get to work from home on Mondays and Fridays![4]

As remote-working leaders, we have to constantly keep abreast of these changes and mold ourselves to the demands of the labor pool if we want to be as effective as possible. For some of us, this might even mean changing cherished parts of ourselves and rethinking our most important abilities. In this chapter, I'm going to examine how remote work changes the idea of effective leadership itself, and how we prepare ourselves to face the new challenges associated with this change.

LEADERSHIP EMERGENCE IN VIRTUAL ENVIRONMENTS

As we move into a world where virtual environments become the norm, the kind of qualities that people look for in a leader also begins to change. Leadership emergence theory (LET) can tell us a little bit about how these priorities are changing in workers. LET is a field of study with overlaps between psychology, sociology, and management, and as the name suggests, it examines how leaders "naturally" emerge in groups of people when they have no formal title or power within that group. This theory is vital to us because it tells about what people consciously and unconsciously value in any leader.

There are two primary or typical paths by which leaders can emerge within groups: through ascription or achievement. In ascription, leaders arise based on qualities ascribed to them by their fellow team members. People are classified as leaders based on their perceived fit with a leadership "schema" or set of qualities. That is, we value someone as a leader simply because they look and act like one. The values we might see in such a leader include dynamism, extroversion, intelligence, and motivation. This is something we see all the time: in high school student council elections, in the selection of a captain in a pickup basketball game, in moments of crisis in which strangers step up, or even in presidential elections. Simply put, people value charisma, whether they like to admit it or not, or whether they even do it consciously or not! Charisma is a trait deeply tied to the notion of being or becoming a leader.

In the achievement pathway, on the other hand, people are valued as leaders for how much they contribute toward solving team goals or making the achievement of those goals as smooth a process as possible.

Task-oriented team members take on leadership positions, and do so because of their organizational, administrative, and communicative skills. They are valued because of their ability to contribute to a team's mission and to help members complete their tasks efficiently and on time. Charisma doesn't matter as much as their ability to be a team player.

A paper published in the *Journal of Business and Psychology* in 2021 looked at how leaders emerge in remote-working environments or different "virtuality contexts."[5] The study involved eight hundred students divided into teams of four or five members. Each team was given the exact same task to perform over a fixed number of sessions over ten weeks and was classified as belonging to a "high," "medium," or "low" virtual environment depending on how *physically* isolated team members were from one another, as well as how much they depended on technology to complete their goals. In high-virtuality teams, for example, members were isolated from one another for the entire duration of the project and were thus heavily dependent on technology for the completion of their tasks.

The study found that in low-virtuality contexts ascription was a far greater factor than achievement in determining leadership emergence, whereas in high-virtuality contexts achievement was far more significant. Why is this the case?

In low-virtuality contexts, or physical offices, most interactions between team members occur face-to-face. In these constant and physical interactions, we're likely to be susceptible to what we call "traditional" leadership traits: we see verbal and nonverbal signals of a person's leadership qualities, namely extroversion, conscientiousness, and intelligence. In an office environment, we're also more susceptible to social cues and are aware of a social hierarchy because of our proximity to other people. We want to interact with and unconsciously admire those team members who are able to command the attention of others. This should come as no surprise. Everyone wants to hang out with the cool kids and, in doing so, also *be* one of the cool kids.

In high-virtuality contexts, on the other hand, we experience new and different challenges because of our spatial isolation and technological dependence. These include temporal and cultural misunderstandings, communication problems, and confusion arising from the difficulty of coordinating tasks. In these environments, we value leaders with the ability to address this confusion, allowing us to complete our tasks with efficiency and ease. Given that we are no longer interacting in person constantly, unconscious cues and social hierarchies also don't matter nearly as much.

We can see the differences between these two approaches to leadership in the words of Jamie Dimon and Frédéric Oudéa. Dimon prioritizes the kind of leadership we ascribe value to, whereas Oudéa wants to promote a kind of leadership that is more oriented toward team members and concerns about *their* issues. As a leader transitioning from an office to a remote-working environment, you might be a little shocked by the differences in these approaches. You might wonder, "Does this mean my charisma and personality don't matter as much as my ability to be some kind of logistical coordinator?"

No, that isn't true. But you're going to have to find a better balance between the two approaches, just as I have in my career, which I will discuss below. I also don't think the divergence of leadership approaches should come as *too* much of a surprise.

I believe this trend of task-oriented and administrative leaders rising over large personalities who lead through sheer charm has been going on for some time now. Take a look at the current CEOs of the largest tech companies in the United States, like Apple, Google, and

Microsoft, and try to figure out what they all have in common (besides brilliant educations and glasses with very thick lenses). I don't mean to suggest that all corporate leadership has changed forever, nor do I mean to suggest that it happened suddenly over a few months. For every Sundar Pichai you will still probably find yourself an Elon Musk. All the same, it is time to think about how leadership is changing as office culture also changes, and what we leaders need to do to ride out these new tides.

STREAMLINING LEADERSHIP

When I first moved into a remote-working position, years ago now, I was in for a little bit of a rough ride—remote work wasn't nearly as ubiquitous and widespread as it is today. First, I had to learn how to use a whole suite of new software and applications and also learn how to configure my computer and workstation to ensure that all communication happened without any hitches. This part was easy; I've never had trouble following instructions.

Where it got a little more difficult was in the subtle, unconscious changes. I realized it was much harder to communicate my personality over video calls and emails than it was in person. Certain emotions and intonations simply can't be conveyed easily over a digital medium with authenticity, and you simply can't be the same person on video as you are in real life. You have to alter the way you speak and how you approach groups or one-on-one meetings.

This isn't an easy realization for someone who has been a leader in an office, and I want to address that here. Many people think that a leadership personality is an innate talent, but as leaders we know this isn't true. Leadership is a skill that we've nurtured over years, one that we've carefully cultivated through trial and error, and one that has—in time—become a very big part of our total personality. If you're transitioning from an office to a remote-working environment, this is one of the first challenges you're going to face, and you must face it head-on. You must be prepared to change some very cherished parts of yourself.

What made this transition easier for me was the realization that remote working had in fact streamlined my role as a leader by reducing some bloat around the job. While being a leader was an important part of my personality, at the office a lot of my role also involved putting on the appearance of a leader or acting out a part. You have to always be confident, expressive, and extroverted while simultaneously motivating others. In remote work, where you no longer spend hours in constant interaction with other team members, you no longer have to devote as much effort to playing this role. Instead, you can direct your energies toward completing your tasks and making work easier for the rest of your team members. Think of it as a little less bluster and charm, and a little more focus and care for your team.

SOFT SKILLS

Above, I mentioned some changes I had to make to myself as a leader when I transitioned to remote work. These changes involved what can also be called soft skills. "Soft" because they are a little subtler and can't necessarily be learned through a book of instructions (unlike hard skills, which we'll talk about below), but "skills" because they have to be carefully practiced over time if we want to learn how to use them well. Here are some soft skills that I think are essential for all remote-working leaders:

- **Communication:** We've covered the importance of maintaining and improving communication in remote environments at length in the early chapters, but I want to reiterate the point here. As a leader, you have to make up for the loss of communication brought about by the absence of constant in-person interaction. This does *not* mean constantly inundating team members with messages but rather maintaining a stream of communication over the appropriate mediums to ensure that your team members do not feel isolated. Most importantly, this should include giving regular and meaningful feedback and checking in with any team members who are new or are having difficulties transitioning from an office to a virtual environment. As discussed in chapter six, it's also vital that you learn the art of the virtual meeting to ensure effective communication between all team members.

  Working on communication also means working on your own voice to make it more appropriate for a virtual environment. If you usually speak in a manner that prioritizes projection, like I do, or have a booming voice, consider that it might not be necessary to still speak this way if you're talking over video.

- **Organizational knowledge:** When working on a project with a team, we usually delegate individual tasks to each member. In an office, if you ever needed to know which team member was working on a specific task, or who had a specific piece of information, you could quite literally just stand up above your cubicle (or step out of your office) and shout out, "Hey! Who knows or has X?" With remote work, that's no longer possible, and it's incredibly ineffective to email or mass-Slack your team every time you forget who possesses what.

As a remote leader, you need to work on your organizational awareness, in the sense of always knowing where the different parts of your project currently are and what state of completion they are in. While virtual collaboration tools can help you, you have to learn to remember that all the pieces of your puzzle are no longer in one physical location. You need to practice this skill so you can save time and aren't always scrambling to find out where one part of your project is.

- **Transfer of knowledge to coworkers:** From the study on leadership emergence I discussed above, we learned that team members appreciate leaders who help reduce confusion by working on coordinating tasks. As a remote leader, you have to not only work on your own communication with your team members, but also learn how to be a facilitator *between* team members. If you're the only conduit of information between them, tasks are going to progress very slowly and there will likely be miscommunication too. Addressing this will involve learning how to manage each of your team members' egos, as well as getting them to speak to one another without having to check in with you each time.

- **Empathy:** I want to make it clear here that charisma is still important for a leader, even if you're in an all-virtual environment. While charisma may not be as important as it once was, you need to channel the effort you once put into leading your in-office staff into caring for your team members. Never forget that remote work can often be very isolating, even if it doesn't feel that way for you. As a leader, you must always work to reduce the feeling of emotional or physical distance between employees, even if they're continents apart. Communicate with them often and meaningfully, and make them feel noticed by recognizing their achievements and efforts.

HARD SKILLS

I want to also briefly go over the hard skills you need and note that though they might seem easier to learn than the soft skills above, this doesn't necessarily make them any less important to your functioning as a remote leader. They are:

- **Proficiency in new software and technology:** It's vital that you keep abreast of all the new software and technological changes that remote work requires in your office. You need to able to lead from the front, showing your team members how to most effectively use new programs and applications. Not doing so will hamper your team's ability to complete tasks efficiently. Additionally, remember that your team members are also learning and getting used to all sorts of new technological changes. Doing your part to learn new information shows them you are in the trenches with them, creating a sense of solidarity between you.

- **Language, cultural, and geographical awareness:** The mass adoption of remote work enhances your ability to hire workers from all over the world. This also means attracting new hires with various linguistic, religious, and potentially even geographical backgrounds. As a leader you want to be sensitive to the diversity these new hires bring to your office. I don't mean to suggest that you learn a new language every time you hire someone from a different country, but it helps to be aware that some of your team members think differently than you do and may also have a different sense of what is and isn't appropriate in workplace relationships. If you hire workers internationally, also keep in mind any time difference. They're not going to be very happy team members if they are waking up at 3 AM for a meeting every week.

- **New management methodologies:** I'm a big fan of management books, and many of the skills I use have been learned from the best authors of the genre. As we continue to learn about remote work and how to best approach it, the literature on the subject is going to grow, and our learning will grow alongside it. As a leader, you have the responsibility to keep abreast of the changes in what we might call the "standard" approach to work, and you're already doing your part by reading this book!

Finally, if you're reading this around the time it's published in 2022, remember that you're at the forefront of the first generation that is adopting remote work as a worldwide standard. You are also going to be the first leaders learning the best (and worst!) practices of remote work, and as such, you must pass on that knowledge to the next generation. If it's in your power to do so, always play the role of mentor to your junior coworkers. They're going to take the reins from you one day, and it will help both them and your company immensely if they're able to do so with confidence and with adequate knowledge of how best to be a remote leader.

LEADERSHIP METHODS: A CONVERSATION WITH CHELSEA ACOSTA PATEL

I want to end this chapter a little differently. So far, I've been concluding with my own methods that I've found have helped me immensely in being a successful remote-working leader. Here, I want to broaden the perspective of the book by turning to a remote leader who has been successful in a location and corporate environment very different from mine, to see what she has to say about remote work, how she is adapting to it, what her notions of remote leadership are, and what her tips and tricks are.

My friend Chelsea Acosta Patel is currently the head of customer experience at Wally Health, a Boston-based personalized dental health care startup. Wally just raised a seed funding round in December 2020, and Chelsea is one part of a small team of fifteen building an exciting new organization brick by brick. She has also previously worked as a consultant and digital product manager.

Chelsea was a working mother of a six-month-old when she joined Wally full-time in February 2020. At the time, the company was still working out of a shared office. She distinctly remembers ramping-up the office shortly after Valentine's Day, and then going fully remote only three weeks later when the pandemic hit and lockdowns were put in place. The team adapted by using tools that should be familiar to all now—Zoom, Slack, virtual collaboration tools, and so on.

After getting through a few weeks of teething issues (pun intended), Wally Health chose to go fully remote and has remained so even today. It now operates with a hybrid work structure in which team members meet once a month for activities that require being in person and work entirely remotely the rest of the time. These activities are prescheduled and not only serve the purpose of running the business, but also create a space for team members to socialize with one another, build bonds, iron out issues, and align on future goals.

Chelsea enjoys this model and told me over the phone that she would much rather meet occasionally for one week straight than go into the office once a week, every week. It's a curious model, but it has worked for Wally and for Chelsea. In the time since she has joined, she has helped scale the organization, helped hire and manage a growing team, and executed all her projects.

I think Chelsea's example is different from mine and particularly instructive for two reasons: (1) Wally Health is working with a far smaller pool of funds than Rohto is and still adapted to remote working with few hitches, and (2) Chelsea actually thought she was joining a real office environment and then had to adapt her life entirely to remote work in only two weeks. When I asked her how remote work was going for her as a leader now, she told me that Wally has proven that virtual works and that success is simply a matter of taking your skills and leadership style and translating it into different modes, such as fully online, hybrid, and once-a-year company offsites. She told me that as a leader, you just need to apply your skills to a digital medium, and that requires some experimenting. She's incredibly confident.

Like me, Chelsea also worked doubly hard over the past year to maintain and build the trust she has with her team—she had no other choice, because she was new to the team. For her, not being able to just physically go to her team members' desks or go out for coffee or lunch in different settings was the biggest change that she had to adapt to, as this was the method she had used in the past to engage with her team members and learn about the kind of leadership they best responded to. Chelsea replaced these sessions with consistent one-on-one Zoom calls with different members of Wally, in which she tries to connect with them on nonwork matters before work starts.

She also doesn't believe that leadership changes too much when a leader goes from an in-person to a virtual office—it just has to be adapted. Central to her notion of virtual leadership is maintaining clear communication. Leadership, as Chelsea explains, is the same whether you're at home or in the office, and she says one of your primary skills is being able to communicate so people know what you're actually thinking. This means reaching out to people actively without making them feel like you are prying or micromanaging, and also having authentic conversations in which they learn about you and you learn about them.

Because Wally is a startup rather than a company with years of established experience, there were details about company policy, culture, and goals that had to be determined when the pandemic hit. Very early on, Chelsea and other Wally leaders realized that much of culture building is simply conversation and discussion based (that is, informal). Unlike in her previous corporate roles as a product manager and management consultant, Chelsea had to have many strategy alignment sessions with her team to replace impromptu and spontaneous in-person meetings, which were out of the question because they were working remotely. Wally's leaders identified the importance that these informal interactions can have for a company, especially a new one, and sought to replace them.

Many of these strategy alignment and vision-planning meetings involved abstract discussions about the company and its goals. Chelsea realized that the team members needed to write down these goals clearly and explicitly and then reference and circulate them frequently throughout the startup—material like this had to be seen and thought about by the whole team. Essentially, there needed to be some kind of visual or textual reinforcement for team members to consistently refer to as they built the company culture.

To make working sessions more vibrant, lively, and effective, Chelsea and her company took full advantage of alternatives to physical whiteboards, such as Google Slides, Notion, and Figma; sometimes participants even quickly illustrated ideas on the fly on a shared PowerPoint presentation.

Chelsea has also taken the lead in getting her team in deeper communication with company stakeholders. After all, customers, other vendors, and dentists are all online now and easily accessible. Wally evolved far more quickly because it opened up virtual mediums to conduct customer interviews or talk to dentists. She says that leaders have to change their mindset because the whole world is fully digital now, and consequently accessible too. Put differently, when taking your team remote, don't try to come up with a company policy in isolation.

Remember that the world around you is also increasingly turning to a remote-first environment, and adjust your policies accordingly.

Chelsea gave me her own list of must-dos for every digital leader:

- In order to lead others, you must first find ways to make remote work *work* for you. You can't create a company-wide policy before figuring out the rituals that matter to you and how you might take them online yourself.

- In meetings, make sure everyone turns their videos on at the very beginning, even if you don't need it later. This adds an element of human contact and connection in which you make yourself vulnerable and not hidden, and if videos are not necessary for the meetings, you can turn them off after your initial and informal interactions.

- Build psychological safety with your team. Chelsea explained this idea as making a space where people can share their ideas and comments freely and openly. As a leader, you need to enable and empower people to be themselves and be more vocal, and you can do so by hosting informal meetings where anything can be discussed or encouraging team members that you perceive as quiet in meetings to speak up and not be shy.

- If you're going hybrid, think hard about the kind of structure and schedule that best suits your company. Wally Health came to its decision only after long discussions with the team and careful consideration of what it needed to function effectively.

- And for mothers-to-be or female readers thinking about juggling remote work with motherhood, Chelsea offers this advice: find the right combination of the things you need to juggle both parts of your life adequately, and then be vocal about it. This might mean articulating to your partner that you need an hour or two to yourself early in the morning, or just being completely offline at a certain time in the evening to read a nighttime story to your child.

CHAPTER 9

THE NEW EMPLOYEE

NEW HIRES AND THE POTENTIAL OF HYBRID WORKSPACES

In May 2021, as vaccines started rolling out in the United States and it started to seem as if the pandemic was under control, the *Washington Post* published an editorial by Catherine Merrill titled "As a CEO, I Worry About the Erosion of Office Culture with More Remote Work."[1] Merrill is the publisher of *Washingtonian*, a magazine published in Washington, DC, that covers local journalism, real estate, and politics.

In the article, Merrill laments the slow return to regular office work, saying that she is "concerned about the unfortunately common office worker who wants to continue working at home and just go into the office on occasion." She lists several reasons why she believes in-person offices are irreplaceable, many of which will be familiar to you at this point, like a lack of socialization, poor communication, and even the fear of missing out (or FOMO, as it's more colloquially known).

At one point, however, Merrill goes on to say the following, perhaps a little threateningly:

> *While some employees might like to continue to work from home and pop in only when necessary, that presents executives with a tempting economic option the employees might not like. I estimate that about 20 percent of every office job is outside one's core responsibilities—"extra." It involves helping a colleague, mentoring more junior people, celebrating someone's birthday—things that drive office culture. If the employee is rarely around to participate in those extras, management has a strong incentive to change their status to "contractor." Instead of receiving a set salary, contractors are paid only for the work they do, either hourly or by appropriate output metrics. That would also mean not having to pay for health care, a 401(k) match and our share of FICA and Medicare taxes—benefits that in my company's case add up roughly to an extra 15 percent of compensation. Not to mention the potential savings of reduced office space and extras such as bonuses and parking fees.*

The article generated a furor and had over five thousand comments on the *Washington Post* website alone. People criticized what they saw as a veiled threat to *Washingtonian* employees in the part about contractors, and also challenged the notion that remote work was just something temporary and could not compete with in-person offices. They didn't believe particularly strongly in Merrill's comments in favor of offices either. As one commenter wrote, "Birthdays? Who cares, I'm here to work, not socialize."

The criticism grew when *Washingtonian* employees themselves condemned the article publicly. Many took to Twitter, including senior editors, publishing a joint message that said:

> As members of the Washingtonian editorial staff, we want our CEO to understand the risks of not valuing our labor. We are dismayed by Cathy Merrill's public threat to our livelihoods. We will not be publishing today.

Merrill eventually posted an apology for her statement, making a particular note about not changing any staff to freelancers, but still maintained that she was worried about what would happen to office culture if remote work was to be more than temporary.

As remote leaders, there's a lot for us to parse out in this article. While Merrill may have voiced her concerns using perhaps poorly thought-out justifications, her concerns are certainly some that I have thought about myself. Even more telling, however, are the reactions of both the general public and the *Washingtonian* employees. Many clearly saw the flexibility and freedom offered by remote work as a newfound gift that they absolutely did not want to give up. Additionally, some employees also feared for their safety (given that the pandemic was still ongoing at the time) but did *not fear* being cowed by their employer. They were able to organize themselves collectively and express their opinions on Twitter—the most public forum of all.

This is a kind of power shift that I've been noticing recently, in which skilled employees are slowly gaining more power over corporations, employers, and public opinion. More than ever before, we're entering a world where the market for skilled work is far more of a seller's market than a buyer's. The onset of the pandemic and the explosion of remote work have only sped up this process further, as workers become more skilled, are able to work from anywhere, and realize that there might actually be more to life than going to a dreary office for forty hours a week.

A new kind of employee is entering the fray, and as managers who are either entering or transitioning to remote work, we need to prepare ourselves to approach them in a manner that is slightly different from what we're used to. They have more say in where they would like to work, the kind of work they would like to do, the kind of perks a workplace should offer, and even the kind of managers whom they would like to be overseen by.

For managers, this new generation of workers can be a boon if used well: they're more skilled than ever and more invested in working for companies they care about and identify with, rather than just where they can earn their next paycheck.

Who are these new employees? And how can they be best integrated into a world where remote working is the norm?

WHAT'S NEW?

These trends in employee behavior aren't particularly new, but they have been accelerating recently. Technology has played a large part in this, and the advent of widespread remote work has only furthered the change. Here are some of the new characteristics that I see in the next generation:

- **They are more skilled than ever:** Workers now have access to more free resources for education and upskilling than ever before. They're trained to be adaptable and can be used in several different positions—they even desire the kind of variety and multidisciplinary learning that working in different departments offers.

- **They have nontraditional educations:** Four-year degrees are no longer the norm for workers who wish to be hired at the world's leading and most competitive workplaces. In fact, in 2019 half of Apple's US hires did not have a four-year degree.[2] Workers are able to learn skills without the need of formal classrooms and, in certain cases, can even learn skills that aren't usually taught in colleges. Consequently, these workers also tend to have different expectations of what an ideal workplace looks like and different expectations for what constitutes success at work.

- **They have different cultural backgrounds:** Minority groups and immigrants continue to grow in number at the workplace, and they can also have different norms about what constitutes appropriate workplace behavior, about what success looks like, and even about their ideal boss or manager.

- **They have new ideas about the workplace:** A fat paycheck, a new MacBook, and a plush Herman Miller chair are no longer sufficient perks to address the best talent (though I do believe they will still work most of the time). According to Deloitte's 2021 Global Millennial Survey, Millennials want to work at companies that contribute to the greater good of society, care about (and actively demonstrate their practice of) diversity and inclusion principles, and are invested in the mental well-being of their workers, among other factors.[3]

- **They want to work from anywhere:** The sudden adoption of remote work during the pandemic showed both workers and workplaces that it was far easier to work from anywhere than previously thought. Even after the pandemic was under control, many workers did not want to return to the old normal. A large-scale study by the software company Citrix found that "83% of employees think that workers will be more likely to move out of cities and other urban locations if they can work remotely for a majority of the time, creating new work hubs in rural areas."[4]

- **They have new ownership of time:** The sudden shift to remote work has also resulted in a new understanding among employees about their ownership of time. The absence of rituals like commuting and other in-person activities means that remote workers have more time to pursue other activities like taking care of their family or even taking up a hobby. As many offices try to return back to "normal" in-person environments, many workers are likely to be reluctant to give up this newly found sense of ownership.

- **They desire flexibility:** Workers want flexibility in terms of both *where* they work and the *time* they have to work. They want to prioritize their lifestyle and family over showing up at the same time every day at the office.

- **They seek a community:** Workers want to be a part of a workplace where employees feel connected to one another, with shared visions of their tasks, their goals, and, more broadly, what an ideal society should look like. Simply put, they desire workplace relationships that are substantial and give them a reason to go to work every day.

- **They know what they want:** To go back to the anecdote at the beginning of this chapter, workers are also more powerful and better organized than prior generations have been. They demand more from the companies they work for, they are willing to hold their leaders and managers accountable, and they are *not* willing to remain silent in the face of what they perceive as injustices in the workplace.

- **They can be picky:** All of this is to say that the best workers are pickier than ever before! They demand more from their workplaces and hiring offers and can afford to do so because they have the skills to back themselves up.

ADDRESSING EMPLOYEES' CONCERNS AS THE WORLD RETURNS TO NORMAL

Looking at the list above can be a little daunting, but keep in mind the following: (1) it would be close to impossible to address every single one of these points, especially at one go; and (2) workers who are both more skilled and more invested in their work are nothing but good news for team leaders.

Many of the concerns of these new employees can be addressed by creating an empathetic office culture where workers are invested in their work, feel like they share the company's goals, and also feel seen by managers and leaders. How do you do that, you ask?

Well, you read the rest of this book! That's what we've been trying to address so far, and many of the chapters contain information that will be as useful for office leaders as it is for remote leaders. Changing office culture is a slow process—it requires commitment and time, but it will help you attract the best talent.

Wherever I've worked, I try to lead by example and encourage my employees to emulate my behavior. For example, at Rohto we have comprehensive paid maternity leave. In theory, mothers don't have to worry about taking time off from work when giving birth to and taking care of their newborn. As a mother, however, I know that maternity leave is different in practice. Having a child involves giving up hours of your life that used to be devoted to other things; while this is a blessing, it can also make you feel like you're missing out on things going on elsewhere, especially at work, because a lot can change over a period of weeks or months.

I recognize this fear in myself and try to address it for my team members. Whenever one of them goes on maternity leave, I set up a schedule in which I call them on a regular basis over the period in which they're away or meet them for lunch in person. In these meetings, I not only take the time to discuss their personal life and their child, but also go into depth about what is going on at work and update them on any changes that may be relevant to their position. Rohto also offers its employees on maternity leave online courses to keep them engaged and learning. It's important to make your team members feel like they matter, and all it takes is a little effort on your part.

However, not all concerns can be addressed by culture alone. Solutions may require rethinking the physical and remote offices as mutually exclusive entities. As I write this in the summer of 2021, workers are beginning to return to offices around the globe, and I've already been working at the offices of Rohto for a few months now. However, having had a taste of what freedom from offices looks like, around 70 percent of workers no longer want work to be structured like it was prior to the pandemic (that is, forty to sixty hours a week in the same old dreary office). That leaves a good chunk of workers who *do* want an office and want things to return to what they were. How does a leader address all of this—talented workers with new goals and desires, team members who don't want to go back to the norm, and other team members who do? It can sound like a bit of a mess.

For some companies and offices—those that have the appropriate infrastructure and culture—hybrid offices can be the answer.

WHY HYBRID OFFICES?

Many of the largest organizations in the world are now embracing hybrid workplaces that allow them to combine the best of remote and physical workplaces. In hybrid offices, the time a team member spends working in the office (or other workplace) versus their home is flexible. Some departments might come in on specific days, workers might only come in for meetings, or offices might be open spaces and employees might come in whenever they like. There are countless different combinations of what remote work can look like.

In some offices, hybrid can also mean that only certain kinds of workers come into the office at all, while others can be remote full-time. IT departments, for example, can often be entirely remote.

Some of the advantages of a hybrid model, over both all-remote and all-office work, are that it can help you with the following:

- **Fighting loneliness and dreariness:** As explained at length in chapter five, remote work can be an isolating experience. Having some face-to-face time can keep team members feeling cheery and social and also help leaders identify any indicators of burnout or trouble employees may be experiencing. Additionally, all-remote or even all-office work can grow monotonous over time. Hybrid work can inject a much-needed boost of energy and creativity into your office by dispelling the dreariness of doing the same thing day after day.

- **Keeping all generations happy:** As discussed in the previous chapter, there's a whole generation of business leaders who practice and have been trained in a kind of leadership that is not entirely suitable for remote work. Going hybrid keeps this generation happy by allowing them to practice their skills in an environment that is familiar, while also allowing those who prefer remote work to continue to do as they please from home.

- **Balancing community and freedom:** Hybrid work addresses multiple concerns outlined at the start of this chapter. In-person interactions can help employees build a sense of community with one another and build bonds that are far stronger than those built over Slack, Zoom, and email. At the same time, flexibility with regard to office hours can give employees the time they want and need to work from the comfort of home (or wherever they may be), enjoying their own pursuits or time with their family.

- **Attracting talent:** If you can successfully run a hybrid office in which the advantages outlined above are achieved, then you will also be well on your way to attracting the best talent the next generation has to offer. Additionally, this can also help ensure that you're retaining the best talent you already have in your office. Why would they want to go anywhere else when they have all they need with you? A more loyal and invested staff, and more trust between you and your team, means a far more productive workplace.

THE HURDLES OF GOING HYBRID

I initially thought I was going to title this section "The Disadvantages of Going Hybrid," but thought better of it. There are no general disadvantages that apply to all hybrid offices. There are, however, hurdles to be overcome, and these hurdles vary depending on the kind of office you already work at and what you want to achieve by going hybrid. The hurdles I want to talk about here won't necessarily represent all the challenges of an office trying to move from an entirely physical presence to one that includes remote work—addressing those is the point of the rest of the book.

If you're part of an office that has been remote throughout its existence and you now see the benefits of having some kind of physical workspace, going hybrid will involve a lot of costs. In addition to what your company pays for space and office equipment, your team members are also going to incur costs like transportation, food, and perhaps even new clothing. You may have to provide them with some kind of "transition" budget in order to keep them happy. If your company already has a large office presence, on the other hand, going hybrid will involve a lot of downsizing and rethinking. Remember our discussion of Dropbox in chapter four? When your company no longer needs a full-size office, you will need to think about how you use assets that may not be required for an office that is partially remote.

Requiring your team members to meet together in some kind of physical space also means putting some level of restrictions on where they can live. This can be off-putting for team members and new hires who want flexibility in where they can live, but can be addressed using satellite offices or rental budgets. In addition to renting your main offices, you can rent workspaces in or near cities where a number of your team members live, or you can even provide them with a stipend every month to rent these spaces themselves. This will involve determining both the budget and how many employees are "enough" to warrant a satellite office. Of course, this practice will still involve some restrictions—your team members can't live on the farm in the middle of the boonies or in the Maldives if they have to get to an office near a metropolitan area every day.

Perhaps the main concern of going hybrid is scheduling, in terms of deciding who comes to the office and when. Will you create a system wherein everyone has to come to the office for three days a week and the other two days are remote? Do employees have flexibility in terms of which days they can choose to come in? Or will you create a system in which your team comes into the office only for specific events or meetings? How about a hybrid culture where only some workers need to come in at all, while others are remote full-time? You can even create a system with three categories of workers—full-time office, full-time remote, and hybrid office-remote workers. These aren't easy questions to answer. In fact, they may even be the *main* question. I'll address them in the section below.

If you end up with a model in which only certain teams or departments have to come to the office at all, then you have a few more hurdles to address. Hybrid meetings can be confusing if they are interdepartmental and involve having a certain number of people join from a room while others are on video. Unfortunately, there is no secret to making videoconferences feel like they're physically happening in your room (at least not until augmented reality makes great strides). What you can do, however, is follow the best practices for meetings outlined in chapter six: plan meetings in advance, account for time differences, send out agendas, and keep meetings short and interesting.

Hybrid offices can also encourage an imbalance of power between some of your team members. You will want to ensure that there is no difference in access to resources between your physical and virtual teams. It would be unfair to your workers if being assigned to a remote team meant they did not have access to nearly the same amount of equipment or other resources as your in-office teams. Addressing this might mean providing remote workers with some kind of budget as outlined in chapter four. Similarly, all-remote workers might feel less recognized than their counterparts in the office. As a leader, you can address this by having one-on-one conversations with them constantly, as well as giving them meaningful feedback and making them feel as included in your office culture as possible.

Finally, if you do choose to go hybrid, make sure that your office is serving the purposes it was intended to serve. That is, make sure it emphasizes the human element. Your office should be a place where workers can socialize (to some extent) and take advantage of being face-to-face with one another. To address this, many companies like Google and Facebook are redesigning their workplaces for more socialization. As a leader, you don't even have to go that far. Lead by example and try to create a culture where you are socializing with your coworkers and having authentic and meaningful conversations.

HOW DO I GO HYBRID?

Addressing the hurdles of going hybrid means taking a deep look at your office and determining what hybrid structure works best for you. This is not a one-size-fits-all situation, and as a leader you should be taking stock of your office, team members, and goals before emulating another business's hybrid structure. Here are some guidelines for going hybrid:

1. **Listen to your team and administration:** Create surveys where your team members can express their opinions on hybrid work, what their goals and desires are, and how they perceive themselves as fitting in with your company. Hold one-on-one discussions with team members at different managerial levels, and once you have enough information on what they want, discuss going hybrid with the administrative stakeholders, armed with your data.

2. **Develop joint solutions:** When deciding on a hybrid model, don't pick a solution that favors one team, one managerial level, or even one group of employees. Try to create a solution that takes note of all stakeholders and keeps as many of your workers as possible happy and productive.

3. **Monitor the situation:** Once you've initiated changes, don't just sit back and expect to enjoy the fruits of your labor. Make sure you and your team members are constantly monitoring how the new model has affected workflows, productivity, and satisfaction, and how it relates to burnout.

4. **Allow your model to evolve:** If changes are necessary based on your observations, make sure to update your model constantly. New software, new management techniques, and a whole new generation of employees mean that the only constant in the future of hybrid-remote work is going to be change.

LEADERSHIP METHODS: A CONVERSATION WITH RADHIKA DHOTE

I'm going to end this chapter with another interview, this time with someone who can shed a little more light on what we discussed about the new employee.

Radhika Dhote is a senior manager at Flipkart, India's largest homegrown e-commerce company (Walmart acquired a 77 percent stake in the organization in 2018 for $18 billion), which she joined in mid-2020. Radhika works on Flipkart Quick, the company's recently launched hyperlocal delivery service. Before she moved home to India in early 2020, she worked for Walmart for three years in San Francisco and New York City after graduating from UC Berkeley in 2017.

When I last spoke to Radhika, I called her in London, where she had moved in early 2021 and was working remotely for Flipkart, which is based out of Bangalore. Her team consists of eight people, none of whom she has met in person and none of whom have actually met one another in person. The team was formed remotely and functions entirely remotely. For Radhika and her team, this entirely remote structure hasn't hampered their workflow at all. She wakes up and begins work at 7:30 AM every day, London time, and logs off at around 4:30 PM, although on occasion some small tasks may spill over into the evening. Her team knows she lives in London and tries to work around her schedule, and Flipkart doesn't expect her to move home any time soon.

She does notice the absence of some kind of social aspect at work. There are few opportunities for mentorship (either mentoring or being mentored), and she doesn't have the same kind of bond that she did with her coworkers at Walmart. All the same, her priorities are different at Flipkart. She doesn't see herself staying there indefinitely and rising through the ranks, but instead wants to use her time there to learn what she needs from her role. As such, she doesn't mind the lack of face-to-face interactions with her coworkers.

The freedom offered by the remote office has also given her a completely new perspective on work. She described her lifestyle in New York as being "go-go-go" all the time. Every day, she'd get ready at the same time, go to work and do as much as she could, stay late, and then go out to either dinner or drinks with her coworkers. A day was successful if she packed as much into it as possible, and week-days never offered any respite from this rapidity. She says she never felt like she could slow down, and also that she never imagined herself as a work-from-home person. She believed she needed that pace and packed schedule.

Now that she's had a year of freedom and working from home, she sees things a little differently. Everything is more relaxed, and it feels like she has far more time to herself than she ever did. She also sees her priorities far more clearly now and describes the feeling she has as the one you hope to get from taking a holiday when you're working from an office. You take a holiday to decompress, get a little perspective or distance from what you've been doing, and try to realign your goals and desires. With remote work, you don't need that holiday. The pace of life is so much slower, and you have so much more time to do what you want or need to—like cooking dinner, spending more time with friends and family, and even applying to an MBA program. You can simply be yourself. She describes doing more things now that keep her "healthy, happy, and sane." Radhika also thinks it would have taken her many more years to realize what her priorities were if she hadn't been able to work remotely.

While she does see herself going back to an office at some point in her career, she doesn't see herself going back to a fifty-hour, five-day workweek in an office ever again. For herself, and anyone considering taking on a remote position, she has the following advice for the future: think hard about what you want. If what you're going to learn in the role matters to you more than opportunities to connect and bond with your fellow coworkers, then don't be afraid to take on a fully remote role. On the other hand, if these bonds matter to you—for example, if you're building a startup and cohesion and culture are vital to the success of your company—then you might want to be on a team for which face-to-face time is part of the regular workweek.

Radhika's still figuring out what the future of her own career will look like, but for now she's having a great time working from home in London.

CHAPTER 10

REMOTE WORKING AND THE CHANGING MEANING OF LEADERSHIP

HOW I'VE CHANGED SINCE WORKING ONLINE AND REMOTELY

What comes to mind when you hear the phrase *office culture*, or even *corporate culture*? It's a fairly loaded term, and I find myself thinking about a lot of different things: about the way I dress for work; about the way I lower my voice when speaking in the office; of the respect with which I address my superiors, almost as if they were my elders; and even the jealousy with which I guard my working time, refusing to let anything else spill over into it.

When I flip open the *Financial Times* or even the *Washington Post* during my morning routine these days, I often see an opinion piece or a quote from a business leader about how office culture is being "eroded" by remote work, or how work culture as we know it might be over if we don't return to the office soon.

When these thought leaders talk about office culture, they speak of it in terms that portray it as immutable or fundamentally entrenched, almost as if there were a set of tenets that were passed on to us by our predecessors from centuries ago. The reality, however, is that these ideas are far newer than we're prone to think. The first time the term *office culture* appeared in the *New York Times* was 1987, in a discussion on whether having a computer on your desk makes you appear more or less prestigious.[1]

Notions of what constitutes office culture have also changed over time. Sometimes these changes were dramatic, like when women became a substantial part of the workforce a few decades ago. Sometimes they were minor and cosmetic, like when Silicon Valley, Steve Jobs, and Mark Zuckerberg adopted and made appropriate in the office the "T-shirt, denims, Nikes, and ruffled hair" (one might even say unshowered) look. My point here is that any lamentations for office culture may be both premature and a little misguided. Nothing is dying; work is simply changing.

In this chapter, to reinforce the lessons in earlier chapters and to show how you can put them into practice, I'm going to lay out in greater detail my own experiences as a remote-working leader, the changes in the workplaces I have witnessed, and the ways in which I have had to adapt. You may adapt differently yourself, of course, given your own circumstances, but how you end up isn't as important as getting used to changing your leadership strategies for this moment and in the future.

I don't quite know exactly what work will look like decades from now—robots may have replaced my role by then, or may even have written a book a lot like this one—but being open to change and knowing how to adapt to it is perhaps the most vital skill any future leader can have.

REGAINING TIME

My life as an international business leader at Rohto initially looked a lot like George Clooney's in the movie *Up in the Air*. Almost a third of my life was spent in airport lounges or planes, and I used to fly regularly to multiple countries around the world to meet with Rohto's subsidiary CEOs because not all meetings could happen online. This usually meant two to four international flights in a given week, perpetual jetlag, and a constantly stacked agenda.

About two years ago, I modified my role to make it more remote-oriented to reduce my travel time, and then the onset of the pandemic turned most (if not all) of even my local engagements remote. I thought initially that this would give me far more time to do the things I'd like, but what happened in reality was a little different. I found that I became, strangely enough, both freer and far busier.

There were no more hour-long drives to the airport, no more hours of waiting in the lounge before boarding, no more whole days in the air. All my newfound time allowed me to take better care of myself and the friends and family members whom I am closest to: I was going to the gym more, attending more social gatherings, and spending more time with my daughter. I was also more available to my work team for meaningful conversations and good discussions.

All this newfound time, however, seemed to have come at the price of a more compressed or dense workday. I still found myself in consecutive meetings with international leaders whom I would have been visiting otherwise, and I was frequently switching from one meeting room to another in the blink of an eye with no time for a quick break. In fact, I found myself in *more meetings* than ever before, simply because there was a greater need to stay aligned with the other virtual leaders of my company.

I find this change quite paradoxical, in that time has both been saved *and* lost. But in a way, this change is quite characteristic of remote work in general, because there are always trade-offs along the spectrum from being fully remote to being in an office full-time. For me, addressing this meant figuring out how I could best make remote work *work* for me—you may notice that Chelsea Acosta Patel also stressed this in her interview above.

How did I do it?

Well, it wasn't easy, and unlike many of you, I had the chance to figure my routine out over years, not weeks or even days. I made my role leaner: I cut out any superfluous roles I had to play or tasks I had to do and delegated those roles to subordinates in my company. As head of international business development, I also delegated more responsibilities to my regional CEOs, allowing them to take on the roles that I would often play when I would travel abroad for marketing and sales meetings. Perhaps the most important part of delegating responsibilities was creating a channel of communication between these CEOs. By working together and sharing materials with one another, they not only improved our business but also took a heavy load off me.

Having even more time on my hands after these changes means that I've also been able to pursue other simultaneous opportunities along with my day job. Thanks to Rohto's policy of allowing all employees to work on side projects, I've been privileged to pursue my own passion of establishing a news media website called Intech.Media (which can be visited at www.intech.media) while also consulting for Morisawa, an established typography company in Japan.

Making remote work "work for you" really means reassessing your own role and trying to take advantage of what this new work environment can offer. This also applies to how you approach your team.

MAKING THE MOST OF DIFFERENT PERSONALITY TYPES

In the course of this book, I've discussed at length the importance of empathy for those you work with and those you work for. It's an important quality that enables trust and paves the way for setting your company up for success in a remote and hybrid working world. It involves a combination of imagination and listening, in which you try to put yourself in your coworkers' shoes to understand their motivations and how you can best help them be productive and inspired.

For me, empathizing as a remote leader also meant discovering a new kind of balance I had to maintain. How could I help my team members thrive and be comfortable, while also prioritizing the success of my company as a whole? After all, I was brought in to boost Rohto's sales, not to make sure everyone was happy. The short answer is that it involved making difficult decisions.

Many of the members of my team were not suited to remote work, and I don't mean those team members who were laid off during the pandemic. Not everyone is suited to the kind of virtual communication and collaboration that remote work demands: some people struggle with emails, virtual calls, and motivating themselves while working alone.

On the other hand, many of my team members thrived in remote-working environments. Workers who were formerly quiet and reluctant to participate in discussions in the office now found their task-oriented work style valued. Being an empathetic leader in this situation meant recognizing why these workers were succeeding, delegating more work to them given that they were clearly able to handle it, and, when appropriate, promoting them for the value they were adding to my team.

In some cases, I was also able to transfer workers to different departments that they were better suited to. Admittedly, this happened rarely, but it was yet another case of trying to identify what a worker was good at. We had someone working in our administrative team who was going to be laid off under our new remote-working rules. I was reluctant to let him go because I saw the value he was adding to our internal meetings over Zoom. He was a joy to fellow coworkers and facilitated a kind of social bonding. Realizing the importance of this skill and how rare it can be, I transferred him to a client-facing team where he now interacts with our clients in video meetings, and the move was a success.

There are clearly ways to optimize work for your individual team members without sacrificing the greater good of productivity and sales (or whatever metrics are relevant at your company). The unfortunate flip side of this, if you're in a business transitioning from an office to remote work, is that some of your team members may be unsuited to their new roles. Do your best to help them adapt to the new situation, have honest conversations about what going remote entails, and make the difficult decisions when—and only if—you have to.

LEADING WITH DIVERSITY AND INCLUSION

Diversity matters, and it's great for companies too! A large-scale study by McKinsey found that ethnic and gender diversity contributes positively to a company's profitability, but also that women and minorities remain drastically underrepresented.[2] This matters to me a lot, especially as a single mother. I do what I can to help the women in my company, whether it's having one-on-one office hours with team members or keeping new mothers in touch with what is going on, but individual efforts can only go so far. It really is on you, as a leader, to help create systemic change, and I don't see why anyone should avoid doing so, especially because it's proven to be an advantage to companies. It can make your company more profitable, it helps your company attract a wider pool of talent, and it makes everyone on your team feel like they belong.

Admittedly, ethnic and racial diversity isn't as much of a concern in Japan as it is in the rest of the world, but I still try to ensure that the organizations I'm associated with do their best to create equal opportunities for those from different backgrounds. Practices to promote diversity must always start with the recruiting stage. When hiring for my team, I try to use compensation modeling that avoids any biases in race or gender and adjusts for the location and associated cost of living of the worker being hired. Additionally, when I interview potential new team members, I always look for those who can add something to my team rather than just fit in. Many recruiters swear by the approach of "good versus bad fits," but I believe it's a restrictive model that can blind you to good, new talent.

After I've hired a new team member, I then make sure to take the necessary steps to get them acclimated. After their orientation, I work with our HR team to ensure that they receive any new training and free access to online resources that they need, and when possible, I also try to get them tools like laptops or wireless equipment if they need those.

Take the time to look for talent outside the bounds of your own expectations, and once new employees are hired, put in the effort to get them up to speed with the rest of your team. Whenever I've hired a talent that hasn't quite "fit," I've always found that they've added something new and valuable to my team.

TAKING ADVANTAGE OF THE POWER OF THE INTERNET

One of my greatest joys in going remote is the ability to complete tasks more quickly with the help of the internet. Across both my work at Rohto and my side projects with Intech.Media, I have been able to identify and work with digital vendors halfway across the world for various projects, all from the comfort of my home office. I've learned that there are some incredibly powerful and specialized digital services available online, and these organizations are only growing with time.

In fact, collaborating with these other agencies has allowed me to expand my own work's reach and impact to different countries. For example, Rohto's push to go remote has also coincided with my team's use of more third-party marketing firms in our various regions, allowing us to develop campaigns that are better targeted to the local populations.

While these services were also available before my full transition to being a virtual leader, I believe that using them was possible for me only because I developed a remote-first mindset that pushed me to find solutions and creative work-arounds to job issues in the online world. Need an app developed quickly? Need a new logo for a pilot project? Need to learn French to try to impress a new client? Solutions to *all* needs are more abundant than ever before.

Another way to get introduced to new forms of technology is by reaching out to your team. Let them know that you're open to digital alternatives to the status quo and open to their researching and trying new platforms. I once tried this with my team and found that my teammates were incredibly enthusiastic about technological solutions that I had never heard of. This was how our office ended up with an Owl Pro, a smart, connected device with a 360-degree camera and stellar microphones that helps facilitate hybrid meetings by allowing remote-only participants to see everyone in a meeting room at the same time. Frankly, I don't think I would have found out about this device myself. Being open to my team's opinions helped us adopt a piece of technology that made all our meetings a little more enjoyable.

IN CONCLUSION—A FINAL NOTE ON MY METHODS

One of the reasons I wrote this book, or perhaps one of the reasons I believed I had the standing to write this book, was that I had years of experience in remote work prior to 2020 and believed that my knowledge could be useful to the millions of new remote workers and leaders created by the pandemic. Hopefully, I've imparted that knowledge to you in the previous chapters, and my confidence in myself was rightly placed.

What I tried to convey with this final chapter was not only my expertise but also my ability to adapt. More than any other skill, adaptation is central to the remote-working leader of the future. Since the beginning of the pandemic, we have witnessed amazing strides in technology and lasting changes in the culture of work as a whole, and there appears to be no sign of these changes slowing down.

The generation of workers that is currently entering the workforce epitomizes this change. The so-called Gen Z approaches technology with a comfort, understanding, and interconnectivity that I can't even imagine. I've had the pleasure of hiring some of them at Rohto recently and also work remotely on my media projects with two young workers from India and China—both of whom I have never even met in person. I'm constantly learning from these young people about new trends in technology in media and enjoy these interactions as learning experiences.

As a remote-working leader, you will find that this kind of learning is available to you everywhere, as long as you're open to it. Remote work might seem like the future for now, but our visions for the future can change as quickly—or even more quickly—than our immediate present can. If you don't believe that, just take yourself back to the world before the pandemic and try to imagine almost a fifth of the world's workforce adapting to remote work in a matter of months.

I hope my book has provided you with some insight into the world of work that awaits, and I wish you the best in helping your company transition to a remote or hybrid workplace with you, a virtual leader, championing the process.

EPILOGUE

TAKEAWAYS

Whenever I finish a meeting, take a class, or am in a position where I've just learned something new, I immediately create a summary of my learning when I'm alone. It's a simple exercise, and it helps me absorb what I just heard or saw with a little more clarity.

The short chapter summaries below are not intended to be replacements for everything I've talked about in this book. I'm afraid that you're actually going to have to read the book to learn anything of importance. Instead, these succinct summaries consist of five key takeaways from each chapter that will hopefully reactivate in your mind the things that you read, and thus help engrave the concepts into your mind. This also serves as a kind of directory for when you want to find something specific in the book.

CHAPTER 1: THE THREE PLACES

Don't underestimate the importance that rituals play in all parts of your life, including work. They help provide order, continuity, calm, and even joy. We can often overlook rituals because they're so embedded in our lives.

When transitioning to a virtual office, you have to lead the effort to reintroduce rituals that were part of your regular office. This includes both your individual rituals and those that are common to your coworkers.

In order to learn what rituals matter most to you and your office, make a note of what you do hour by hour in the office in a week, and take a look at agendas from previous weeks, making note of any rituals that pop up constantly.

Not all rituals can be transferred online, but many rituals that you might think do not make sense in a virtual environment can be transferred—if you take the effort to lead by example and perform them with authenticity.

Remember that virtual work has collapsed the delineations between "home" and "work."

CHAPTER 2: TRUST IN THE REMOTE WORKPLACE

Trust is the bedrock of the office—both virtual and physical—and is necessary for good communication, morale, positive working relationships, and the overall productivity of your workplace.

There are barriers to trust that are endemic to both virtual and physical offices, but isolation and reliance on technology can make problems worse in the former: distractions, miscommunication, and burnout are rampant.

Overmonitoring your team members using new technology is not the answer when you feel like you're no longer getting the most out of your team. It can make them feel watched and harangued.

Instead, focus on fixing the way you communicate with your team by encouraging more open communication and creating a culture of meaningful feedback.

Practicing an inclusive form of leadership in which your team has a say in the decisions you make, as well as giving high-performing team members access to informal leadership, can also encourage more trust in your office.

CHAPTER 3: FORMS OF COMMUNICATION IN THE REMOTE WORLD

In the remote world, communication is no longer synchronous. Responses are no longer as immediate as they were when we worked in an office with cubicles, and leaders have to get used to this new normal.

Leaders must keep abreast of new tools that are constantly being developed to make the most out of remote work: apps like Slack and visual collaboration tools have made remote work easier than ever before.

To make the most of a plethora of different communication media, determine what kind of communication you use each different app for. Reduce bloat by making strict rules about what goes where, and disseminate them to all your team members to make sure that everyone sticks to the guidelines.

If you run an international office, or one across different time zones, always make sure that all team members are aware of the time differences so you don't have to attend (or have one of your team members attend) a meeting at, say, 2 AM.

Even though your office is now online, make sure to create avenues for informal communication. This might involve *formalizing* informal communication, but all the same, doing so is vital to maintaining a vibrant and innovative office.

CHAPTER 4: REINVESTING YOUR SAVINGS

For companies, going remote is also a chance to go leaner. But all those savings only make sense if you reinvest in your company's most valuable resource: your team.

Reinvesting in your team encourages trust and is beneficial for both you and your team. Upskilling your employees and providing them with office equipment can increase your overall productivity, as well as make them more likely to feel invested in the future of your company.

Consider reinvesting in your team to create a good reputation for yourself. This will help you attract the best talent in the future.

To determine how and how much to reinvest, have a discussion with your company's administration and HR team. Then create a hierarchy of different avenues for reinvestment based on how valuable they will be for your team.

Once you have earmarked funds for more vital reinvestments, like equipment and upskilling, then consider using any extra funds for making work more fun or exciting for your team.

CHAPTER 5: MENTAL HEALTH IN THE REMOTE WORKPLACE

Burnout is now more common than ever, especially since the world has gone remote. Being socially isolated, remaining online all the time, and overworking can all contribute to poor mental health.

As a leader, you have to be vigilant about identifying signs of poor mental health in your team. This may be hard to do, especially if you're always online. Look for signs of reduced productivity, notice when team members are working far too late, and keep an eye out during video calls for anyone who looks particularly tired or disconnected.

Addressing mental health at work means creating a positive work culture. Rituals are central to mental health; make sure to bring them online. Also, consider instituting "mental health days," and have one-on-one sessions with your team members so they can give you meaningful feedback on how they're doing.

Promote self-care among your team members and lead by example. Also, do not underestimate the role physical well-being plays in mental health, and do what you can to keep your team physically healthy. Providing them with gym memberships might be one solution.

As a leader, you should not prioritize your team members' productivity and happiness over your own! Make sure to take care of yourself, note any signs of burnout, and address them as quickly as possible.

CHAPTER 6: THE MEETING

Meetings are supposed to serve the same purpose in virtual offices as they did in real offices, but data show we're having more meetings than ever before. We may be having too many meetings because of all the communication that is lost when we're no longer seeing each other in person.

Always know when not to have a meeting: when there is no agenda, when participants are not given sufficient time to prepare, when no visuals are necessary, and when the meeting would be just for a status update.

As a leader, you need to make sure you're prepared for your meetings. Always make sure your technology is working properly and you have all the software you need, make sure you have all your notes and necessary files in advance, double-check the time and date the day before, and make sure you look your best.

During the meeting, always take notes and try to keep everyone as engaged as possible. If you're having a long meeting, make sure to take breaks so no one is falling asleep or feeling too tired. And as far as possible, always end meetings when they're supposed to; never go overtime.

After your meeting, take some time alone to rehash what you've learned and note down the key takeaways. If your meeting was not as productive as you wanted it to be, reach out to attendees for feedback on what went wrong.

CHAPTER 7: ON MINIMIZING DISTRACTIONS

Working from home means that distractions are going to be a given, and it will pay off if you take some time to identify what these distractions are. A lack of focus can not only affect productivity but also make work far more stressful than it needs to be.

Create an environment for yourself that is conducive to productivity. Get yourself a good chair, make sure your monitor is at an appropriate height, and always try to maintain good posture.

Minimize distractions that nag at you throughout the day. Take walks to combat procrastination, finish household chores at the start of your day, and consider deleting work apps from your phone to stop notifications from distracting you.

Time blocking is an effective technique to manage distractions. When you use it, mark off portions of your day for specific tasks, and do not do anything but what you have assigned yourself to do during that specific period.

If you find yourself feeling particularly distracted and unable to focus, this may be because you are overworked. Always know when to stop. If you start work too early or are working too late, you may end up with diminishing returns in the form of poor focus.

CHAPTER 8: THE NEW LEADER

Virtual environments require a new kind of leadership. Leaders are no longer valued as much for their charisma or personality as they are for how they address the problems that arise in virtual environments.

While this may mean letting go of some of the more cherished notions you have about your own leadership, you can also think if it as reducing bloat. You no longer have to worry about putting on the "face" or personality of a leader, but can instead focus on the actual problems faced by your team.

Remote work demands new soft skills of leaders. You have to be more empathetic, better skilled in communicating, and more organized.

There are also hard skills to be learned: you need to be fluent with new technology and software, keep abreast of any new management methodologies, and also remain keenly aware of any cultural differences if you begin hiring workers from different ethnic, religious, or national backgrounds.

Finally, don't forget that you're at the forefront of the global adoption of remote work. In doing so, think of yourself as a guinea pig, as well as a leader who has lessons for the next generation of workers. As far as possible, always try to pass on this knowledge to any incoming team members.

CHAPTER 9: THE NEW EMPLOYEE

The incoming workers of the next generation are more skilled than ever, and they also demand far more from work than any other generation ever did. Remote work has given them a taste of freedom, and they are not willing to give it all up. Work may have changed forever!

Creating an office culture that is open and empathetic is vital to keeping your team members happy. While it's not easy to do, you have to lead by example and hope the rest of your team emulates you.

Hybrid work can combine the best of the physical office with the freedom that remote work provides, but only if it is done well. If you succeed, you can achieve an ideal balance of community and freedom, and even help attract the best new talent to work with you.

Don't underestimate the hurdles to going hybrid. You will have to do a lot of surveys and introspection to determine the model that best suits your organization, and also take steps to address any imbalances that may arise between workers who come in to your office and those who do not.

If you do end up choosing to go hybrid, make sure to discuss it first with all the stakeholders in your office, create a joint solution, implement it, and monitor how everyone is doing. And don't be afraid to modify or evolve your policy to make it even better!

CHAPTER 10: REMOTE WORKING AND THE CHANGING MEANING OF LEADERSHIP

As the world begins to adopt remote working as a normal form of work, don't think of this as a one-time transition. Work can change again as drastically in the future, so remember that the main lesson to take away from all this change is to be adaptable.

As you go remote, you will find that you have both less and more time. You will have more time to do other things, but you may also be packing more into your workday. Make sure remote work is working for you; try to streamline your role as much as possible and get rid of any superfluous duties.

The skills and personality demanded by remote work are different from those demanded in an office. Try to identify the different personality types in your office and make the most of what they have to offer.

Remote work also gives you the chance to hire workers from a range of different countries, ethnicities, and even income groups. Diversity is good for teams and companies and can foster new ideas and even more productivity.

Don't think of new technology as a hindrance to remote working. Things are going to keep changing, and if you can keep abreast of all the changes, the power of the internet and apps will work in your favor.

ACKNOWLEDGMENTS

The first people I would like to thank are my parents. My mother has always supported my dreams, and while my father cannot read this now, I would not be who I am without the two of them and would like to express my deepest gratitude. I'd also like to thank my incredibly powerful, talented, and loving sister, who has always encouraged me. She inspires me with her career as an anesthesiologist and her mastery of Pilates. She holds free workshops for more than 1,000 students each month and I have so much more to learn from her.

If I hadn't worked at Rohto, I wouldn't have dreamed of publishing this book. I would like to thank everyone in the International Business Department for your smiles and inspiring me everyday, and for all the moments we've shared. You have all taught me the joy of working together in every aspect of life, shown me the strength and courage to work hard, and given me all the energy and more during the past few years.

Among everyone at Rohto, I would like to thank Masaya Saito the most. When I told him two years ago that I wanted to write a book, he was very interested and asked me, "What kind of book do you want to write? I would like to read it." That was enough to help me jumpstart my project, and his positive vibes helped me finish this book.

I'm grateful to Stephen, my editor, for his many talents and support in publishing the book. Without him, the contents of my book would have definitely shined less brightly. I wanted to also thank the entire BenBella publishing team. Because of you, my book can be made available in America. You believed in me even when my hands trembled while I signed our contract.

I would like to thank Virsitil and Yuka's team. I am very indebted to you all and you first understood the essence of my mission. You worked on the cover design for this book with magical powers, helped create the website, and always thought one step ahead.

I also appreciate all my professors and classmates from my UCLA-NUS EMBA cohort, who I have remotely learned with and who all have shown me so much about being a virtual leader. I'd also like to say a thank you to my teammates and coach, Nick, from the 2020 MIT–Harvard Medical School Healthcare Innovation Bootcamp for giving me ample inspiration.

Moreover, I am thankful for Morisawa, one of the world's leading font companies that has always inspired me with its unique business model and given me opportunities to learn from a new perspective.

I'd also like to thank my mentors Jaiveer, Kai, and Diane. Jaiveer, you helped me with the dream of publishing a book that was at first only a dream. A person like you is the one who truly changes the world. Kai, when I first met you, I was fascinated by your intellect and the ability to find many solutions to one problem. You have always invited me to tackle challenges and helped me when I needed the most help. Diane, you have always opened your arms and invited me into your home, giving me generous support. You have a very broad and selfless heart and I will never forget my gratitude to you.

Last and most importantly, my daughter Aina. You are the treasure of my life. You believed in me more than I did, and lit a light in me. Because of your happiness, I feel alive from God. Thank you for always bringing me the best kind of happiness. I want to give all my love and gratitude to Aina.

And a little bonus thanks to my two dogs and cat during the writing process. They helped me capture the big ideas and details with each purr and woof.

NOTES

INTRODUCTION

1 Microsoft News Centre UK, "More Than Two-Thirds of Staff Want Flexible Working to Stay, Research Reveals," April 6, 2021, https://news.microsoft.com/en-gb/2021/04/06/more-than-two-thirds-of-staff-want-flexible-working-to-stay-microsoft-research-reveals/.

2 Mercer, "Flexible Working | Mercer," accessed October 6, 2021, https://www.mercer.com/our-thinking/career/the-new-shape-of-work-is-flexibility-for-all-global.html.

3 Gallup Inc., "How Has the Pandemic Affected U.S. Work Life?" Gallup.com, March 17, 2021, https://news.gallup.com/poll/339824/pandemic-affected-work-life.aspx.

4 Bhushan Sethi, "CEO Panel Survey: How Business Can Emerge Stronger," *PWC*, https://www.pwc.com/gx/en/ceo-agenda/ceo-panel-survey-emerge-stronger.pdf.

5   Zoe Schiffer, "Apple Employees Say the Company Is Cracking Down on Remote Work," *The Verge*, July 15, 2021, https://www .theverge.com/2021/7/15/22578804/apple-employees-work-from -home-request-denied-hybrid-model.

CHAPTER 1

1   CIPD, "Coronavirus (COVID-19): Mental Health Support for Employees," accessed October 6, 2021, https://www.cipd.co.uk /knowledge/culture/well-being/supporting-mental-health -workplace-return.

2   Jose Maria Barrero, Nicholas Bloom, and Steven Davis, "60 Million Fewer Commuting Hours per Day: How Americans Use Time Saved by Working from Home," *VoxEU.Org* (blog), September 23, 2020, https://voxeu.org/article/how-americans -use-time-saved-working-home.

3   Paul Smith, "Microsoft Boss Says You Still Need to Commute While WFH," *Australian Financial Review*, September 27, 2020, https://www.afr.com/technology/microsoft-boss-undecided-on -the-post-pandemic-future-of-work-20200927-p55zrg.

CHAPTER 2

1   Gallup Inc., "Succeeding with Remote Work," Gallup.com, accessed October 6, 2021, https://www.gallup.com/workplace /316313/understanding-and-managing-remote-workers.aspx.

2   Lilly Smith, "Zoom Fatigue Is Worse for Women, Stanford Study
    Shows," *Fast Company*, April 15, 2021, https://www.fastcompany
    .com/90625371/is-zooms-ux-sexist.

3   Brian Kropp, "The Future of Employee Monitoring," *Gartner*,
    accessed October 6, 2021, https://www.gartner.com
    /smarterwithgartner/the-future-of-employee-monitoring.

CHAPTER 3

1   Esther Tippmann Gantly and Pamela Sharkey Scott, "Driving
    Remote Innovation Through Conflict and Collaboration," *MIT
    Sloan Management Review*, April 15, 2021, https://sloanreview
    .mit.edu/article/driving-remote-innovation-through-conflict-and
    -collaboration/.

CHAPTER 4

1   Roland Li, "Dropbox Signs San Francisco's Biggest Office Lease
    Ever," *San Francisco Business Times*, October 10, 2017, https://
    www.bizjournals.com/sanfrancisco/news/2017/10/10/dropbox
    -kilroy-sf-largest-office-lease-krc.html.

2   Dropbox, "Dropbox Goes Virtual First," accessed October 6,
    2021, https://blog.dropbox.com/topics/company/dropbox-goes
    -virtual-first.

3   Natalie Gagliordi, "Dropbox Will Lay Off 315 Employees, COO
    to Step Down," *ZDNet*, January 13, 2021, https://www.zdnet.com
    /article/dropbox-will-lay-off-315-employees-coo-to-step-down/.

4   Nicholas Bloom, James Liang, John Roberts, and Zhichun
     Jenny Ying, "Does Working from Home Work? Evidence from a
     Chinese Experiment," *The Quarterly Journal of Economics* 130, no.
     1 (February 1, 2015): 165–218, https://doi.org/10.1093/qje
     /qju032.

CHAPTER 5

1   Chip Cutter, "A Year into Remote Work, No One Knows When to
     Stop Working Anymore," *Wall Street Journal*, March 26, 2021, sec.
     Business, https://www.wsj.com/articles/a-year-into-remote-work
     -no-one-knows-when-to-stop-working-anymore-11616751002.

2   Bamboo HR LLC, "Remote Workers Lost Nearly $10,000 from
     Delayed Promotions in Last Year, New BambooHR Study Finds,"
     June 10, 2021, https://www.prnewswire.com/news-releases/
     remote-workers-lost-nearly-10-000-from-delayed-promotions
     -in-last-year-new-bamboohr-study-finds-301310346.html.

3   Kelly Greenwood and Natasha Krol, "8 Ways Managers Can
     Support Employees' Mental Health," *Harvard Business Review*,
     August 7, 2020, https://hbr.org/2020/08/8-ways-managers-can
     -support-employees-mental-health.

4   Jack Kelly, "Indeed Study Shows That Worker Burnout Is at
     Frighteningly High Levels: Here Is What You Need to Do Now,"
     Forbes, April 5, 2021, https://www.forbes.com/sites/jackkelly
     /2021/04/05/indeed-study-shows-that-worker-burnout-is-at
     -frighteningly-high-levels-here-is-what-you-need-to-do-now/.

CHAPTER 6

1   Chang Chen, "Shocking Meeting Statistics in 2020 (That Will Take You by Surprise)," *Otter.ai* (blog), December 24, 2020, https://blog.otter.ai/meeting-statistics/.

2   Evan DeFilippis, Stephen Michael Impink, Madison Singell, Jeffrey T. Polzer, and Raffaella Sadun, "Collaborating During Coronavirus: The Impact of COVID-19 on the Nature of Work," *Working Paper. Working Paper Series. National Bureau of Economic Research*, July 2020, https://doi.org/10.3386/w27612.

CHAPTER 7

1   Silen, "Silen Create Efficient Workplaces | Office Phone Booth," accessed October 6, 2021, https://silenspace.com/about-us/.

2   Kalev Aasmae, "Back to Work? Why Your Next Office Could Be a Soundproof Pod," *ZDNet*, June 23, 2021, https://www.zdnet.com/article/back-to-work-why-your-next-office-could-be-a-soundproof-pod/.

CHAPTER 8

1   Imani Moise and Stephen Morris, "US and Europe Split on Bringing Bankers Back to the Office," *Financial Times*, May 10, 2021, https://www.ft.com/content/547a4dc2-e11b-4e8f-b526-cbf135ba7b4d.

2   Kate Duffy, "Nearly 40% of Workers Would Consider Quitting If Their Bosses Made Them Return to the Office Full-Time, a New Survey Shows," *Business Insider*, June 2, 2021, https://www.businessinsider.in/policy/economy/news/nearly-40-of-workers-would-consider-quitting-if-their-bosses-made-them-return-to-the-office-full-time-a-new-survey-shows/articleshow/83172982.cms.

3   Andrea Hsu, "As the Pandemic Recedes, Millions of Workers Are Saying 'I Quit,'" *NPR*, June 24, 2021, sec. Your Money, https://www.npr.org/2021/06/24/1007914455/as-the-pandemic-recedes-millions-of-workers-are-saying-i-quit.

4   Julia-Ambra Verlaine and David Benoit, "JPMorgan, Goldman Call Time on Work-from-Home. Their Rivals Are Ready to Pounce," *Wall Street Journal*, July 6, 2021, sec. Markets, https://www.wsj.com/articles/jpmorgan-goldman-call-time-on-work-from-home-their-rivals-are-ready-to-pounce-11625563800.

5   Radostina Purvanova, Steven Charlier, Cody Reeves, and Lindsey Greco, "Who Emerges into Virtual Team Leadership Roles? The Role of Achievement and Ascription Antecedents of Leadership Emergence," *Journal of Business and Psychology* 36 (2021): 713–733, https://doi.org/10.1007/s10869-020-09698-0.

CHAPTER 9

1   "Opinion | As a CEO, I Worry About the Erosion of Office Culture with More Remote Work," *Washington Post*, accessed October 6, 2021, https://www.washingtonpost.com/opinions

/2021/05/06/ceo-i-want-my-employees-understand-risks-not
-returning-work-office/.

2   Lisa Eadicicco, "Apple CEO Tim Cook Explains Why You
     Don't Need a College Degree to Be Successful," *Business Insider*,
     accessed October 6, 2021, https://www.businessinsider.in/apple
     -ceo-tim-cook-explains-why-you-dont-need-a-college-degree-to
     -be-successful/articleshow/68308772.cms.

3   Stephen Lesley, "The Deloitte Global Millennial Survey: A Decade
     in Review" *Deloitte*, n.d., https://www2.deloitte.com/content/dam
     /Deloitte/global/Documents/2021-deloitte-global-millennial
     -survey-decade-review.pdf.

4   Tim Minahan, "What Your Future Employees Want Most,"
     Harvard Business Review, May 31, 2021, https://hbr.org/2021/05
     /what-your-future-employees-want-most.

CHAPTER 10

1   Daniel Goleman, "Desk Tops Tell All," *New York Times*,
     September 13, 1987, sec. Magazine, https://www.nytimes.com
     /1987/09/13/magazine/desk-tops-tell-all.html.

2   McKinsey, "Delivering Growth through Diversity in the Workplace
     | McKinsey," accessed October 6, 2021, https://www.mckinsey.com
     /business-functions/organization/our-insights/delivering-through
     -diversity.

INDEX

A

accomplishment, sense of, 50
accountability, 40–41
achievement pathway to leadership, 126–127, 128
activity, 85–86, 87, 112
adaptability, 11, 65, 168, 177
age. *See also* Gen Z; Millennials
    burnout and, 78
    hybrid offices and, 150
Airtable, 50
alignment, 49, 138
appearance, 97–98, 160. *See also* clothing
Apple, 3
Asana, 50
ascription pathway to leadership, 126–128
attention economy, 107
attitude, during meetings, 114
authenticity, 22
availability, leader's, 57

B

Baby Boomers, 78
BambooHR, 76
banking culture, 123–125
behaviors. *See* rituals
belief, trust and, 29
brainstorming sessions, 104
breathing, 114
Buffer, 74

burnout, 34–35, 38, 74, 76, 77–80, 150, 173. *See also* mental health

C

calm, 14, 20
chairs, 109. *See also* home office
changes, adapting to. *See* adaptability
charisma, 126, 127, 128, 133
children, 79. *See also* distractions; parents
chores, 111, 112, 175
Citi, 125
Citrix, 146
clothing, 112, 160. *See also* appearance
collaborative tools, 52, 53
comfort, 14
communication, 38, 171
    asynchronous, 46, 52, 171. *see also* email
    digital, downsides of, 78
    distractions and, 34
    guidelines for, 52–53
    improving, 131
    informal, 53–55, 172
    instant messaging, 48–49, 52
    leadership and, 137
    meaningful, 39
    media for, 171–172. *see also* technology
    in-person, 47
    poor, 32
    productivity and, 31

project management tools, 49–51, 52
real-time platforms, 48–49
streamlining, 51–53, 55–57
synchronous interactions, 47–48
between team members, 132, 163
training on, 51
trust and, 30, 31, 32–35, 39
community, 150–151. *See also* interactions; office culture; socializing
commute, 19, 63
competition, 32, 81
confidentiality, 24
confusion, importance of addressing, 76
connection, 29, 99–100, 139
connectivity, 65. *See also* home office; technology
ConsenSys, 73–76, 84
continuity, 12, 14
contractors, 142–143
control, shared, 38–39
conversations, 24
coronavirus, 2
corporate culture. *See* office culture
corporate training, 69. *See also* training
COVID-19 pandemic, 2
coworking sessions, 104
creativity, 150
cultural awareness, 134
culture. *See also* diversity
trust and, 33–34
culture building, 138. *See also* office culture

D

deep work mode, 116, 117
delegation, 162–163
Deloitte, 145
desks, 109–110. *See also* home office
Dhote, Radhika, 155–158
Dimon, Jamie, 124, 128
disconnection, 74. *See also* isolation; mental health
distractions, 5, 38, 108, 174–175. *See also* focus; procrastination
communication and, 34
minimizing, 110–113
schedule and, 115–117
in virtual vs. physical office, 63
diversity, 145, 165, 177
Doist, 74
Dropbox, 59–61, 62

E

Economist Intelligence Unit, 60
education, 69–70, 145. *See also* training
efficiency, 31. *See also* productivity

egos, 132
email, 46, 48
best uses for, 52
guidelines for, 53
mental health and, 88
monitoring, 36–37
empathy, 81, 83, 133, 148, 164, 176
employees. *See* team members; workers
emulation, leadership through, 25
energy levels, 43, 79, 100, 118, 120, 150
engagement
feedback and, 39
in remote meetings, 100–101
environment, 108–110, 175. *See also* home office
equipment, home-office. *See* home office
exercise, 85–86, 87, 112
expectation, trust and, 29, 30

F

face-to-face interactions. *See* interactions
family, 79. *See also* distractions; mothers
fear of missing out (FOMO), 142
feedback, 40, 79–80, 82, 131, 171
engagement and, 39
mental health and, 84–85
Figma, 138
Financial Times, 123
flexibility, 4, 146
Flipkart, 155–156
focus, 106, 175. *See also* distractions; productivity
creating space for, 106–107
difficulty of, 107
environment and, 108–110
mental state, 113
minimizing distractions, 110–113
during remote meetings, 113–115
schedule and, 115–117
signing off and, 117–118
of team members, 118–121
FOMO (fear of missing out), 142
freedom, 150–151, 156, 157, 161, 176
freelancers, 142–143
functionalism movement, 109
furniture, 109

G

Gallup, 3
Gen X, 78
Gen Z, 78, 125, 168
GitHub, 46, 74
Google, 27–28
Google Jamboard, 103
Google Meet, 97. *See also* meetings

Google Slides, 138
Google Workspace, 41–42
Great Good Place, The (Oldenburg), 9
greetings, 14
group chats, 49
guidelines, importance of, 25

H
happiness, 13
happy hour, 63–64. *See also* socializing
Headspace, 20
health, mental, 74. *See also* mental health
health, physical, 70. *See also* exercise
hires. *See* team members; workers
holidays, 21–22
home, 10, 24. *See also* place
home, working from. *See* remote work
home office. *See also* remote work
    discussing, 24
    minimizing distractions in, 175
    setting up for focus, 108–110
    subsidizing, 65, 70–71, 110, 120, 172
Houston, Drew, 61
hybrid office. *See* office, hybrid

I
inclusion, 39, 165, 171. *See also* diversity
innovation, 54, 56, 104
instant messaging, 48–49, 52
Intech.Media, 163, 166
interactions, 14. *See also* isolation; office
    culture; socializing
        face-to-face, 3, 60, 127–128, 150
        informal, 54–55
        synchronous, 45–46, 47–48
internet, taking advantage of, 166
interruptions. *See* distractions
interviews, 63
intimacy, 24
introductions, 99–100
investing in employees, 40, 64–71, 172–173.
    See also training
isolation, 5, 29, 66, 74, 79, 133, 173. *See
    also* interactions; mental health
        combating, 150
        importance of addressing, 76–77

J
Japan, 6
Jobs, Steve, 160
Journal of Business and Psychology, 127
joy, 13
JPMorgan Chase, 124

K
keystroke logging, 37
knowledge, organizational, 131–132

L
language, 134
Lazard, 125
leaders, 10–11
    qualities of, 126–129, 133
leadership
    achievement pathway to, 126–127,
        128
    adapting to remote work, 135–140
    ascription pathway to, 126–128
    in postpandemic world, 124–129
    remote work and, 5, 175
    as skill vs. talent, 130
    streamlining, 130
    trust and, 31
leadership emergence theory (LET), 126
learning sessions, 103–104. *See also* training
loneliness, 74, 150. *See also* isolation
loyalty, 66, 67, 71
Lubin, Joseph, 73–74

M
maternity leave, 148. *See also* mothers
McKinsey, 165
meals, free, 71, 120
media. *See* technology
meditation, 20, 113–114
meetings
    agenda for, 94, 101
    appearance for, 97–98
    attitude during, 114
    audio vs. video in, 56, 94
    audio-only, 95–96
    backgrounds and, 98
    best practices for, 94–102, 153
    best uses for, 51–52
    challenges of, 89–92
    cohost for, 98, 101
    connection and, 139
    energy levels, 100
    engagement in, 100–101
    evaluating, 101–102
    focus during, 113–115
    guidelines for, 53, 55–56, 174
    increase in, 92–93
    length of, 96, 101
    preparing for, 97–98
    problems with, 93
    purposes of, 92
    remote work and, 5
    rules for, 99

scheduling, 51, 96
time spent in, 91
unnecessary, 93–94
visuals for, 95
workshops, 103–104
meetings, hybrid, 153, 167
meetings, informal, 104, 139
meetings, one-on-one, 82, 84–85, 87
meetings, stand-up, 57, 94, 102–103
mental health, 113, 173
addressing, 75
burnout, 34–35, 38, 74, 76, 77–80,
150, 173
exercise and, 85–86, 87
feedback and, 84–85
importance of addressing, 76
leader's, 86
productivity and, 81
resources, 84
rituals and, 83
signs of deterioration, 80–82
support, 82–83
work hours and, 81–82
work-life balance, 74, 82, 83, 88, 146
mental health days, 84, 88
mentoring, 156
Merrill, Catherine, 141–143
Microsoft, 2, 20, 46
Microsoft Teams, 49, 102
Millennials, 125
burnout and, 78
career goals, 145–146
Mind Share Partners, 77
minorities, 165. *See also* diversity
mirror anxiety, 35
miscommunication, 5
MIT Sloan Management Review, 54
monitor height, 110
monitoring of employees, 27–28, 29, 35–38,
41–43, 171
morale, 30, 31, 32, 38
Morisawa, 40, 163
mothers, 139–140, 148, 165
multitasking, 113, 115

N

Nadella, Satya, 20
National Bureau of Economic Research, 92
National Labor Relations Board, US, 28
notifications, 113
Notion, 138

O

office, home. *See* home office
office, hybrid, 149–155, 176–177

office, physical
designed for socializing, 154
distractions in, 63
leadership traits and, 127–128
perceived benefits of, 141–143
reluctance to return to, 2, 4, 142–143,
146, 176
return to, 123–125
office culture, 138, 148, 159–160, 176. *See
also* interactions; socializing
office-hour sessions, 57
Oldenburg, Ray, 9, 13
open source, 46
Oudéa, Frédéric, 124, 125, 128
overmonitoring, 35–38, 171
overtime, 63, 71, 120
overwork, 79, 175. *See also* burnout
Owl Pro, 167
ownership, sense of, 50

P

pandemic, 2
parents, 23, 79, 139–140, 148, 165
Patel, Chelsea Acosta, 135–140, 162
personality, 127, 128, 129, 130
personality types, working with, 163–164
place, 9, 10–11, 13, 22–25, 78
pods, 106
policy, developing, 138–139
posture, 108
power
hybrid offices and, 153–154
of workers, 143–144, 147
PowerPoint, 138
privacy, 22–23, 24, 28. *See also* trust
procrastination, 34, 38, 107, 108, 111, 175.
See also distractions; focus
Procter & Gamble, 102
productivity, 3, 31. *See also* focus
burnout/stress and, 34–35
distractions and, 34
diversity and, 178
mental health and, 81
remote work and, 4, 63
trust and, 30–31
progress tracking, 50. *See also* status updates
project management tools, 49–51, 52
PWC, 3

R

real estate, 59–61, 62
reciprocation, trust and, 29–30
recognition, 43
reinvesting in employees, 64–71, 172–173.
See also training

relationships, 27, 41, 147. *See also* interactions; trust
relocation costs, 63
remote work, 3–4. *See also* home office
    adapting to, 11, 60–61, 135–140
    advantages of, 61
    concerns about, 5, 124
    endurance of, 3
    experience with, 5
    helping workers adapt to, 74–75
    reluctance to give up, 2, 4, 142–143, 146, 176
    workers unsuited to, 164–165
    workers' view of, 125
Remote-how Academy, 74–75
reskilling, 67. *See also* training
results, 31. *See also* productivity
retention, 67
rituals, 10, 32, 63, 139, 170
    abandoning, 11, 15
    adapting to different places, 11
    commute, 19, 63
    delineation of place and, 13, 22
    encouraging, 15–16
    focus and, 112, 117
    holidays and, 21–22
    identifying, 16–17
    importance of, 12–16
    invisibility of, 12
    maintaining authenticity of, 18–19
    mental health and, 83, 173
    organization and, 14–15
    replicating online, 16–22
    reporting energy levels, 120
    signing off, 83, 88, 117–118
    social interactions and, 14
    work-life balance and, 82
Rohto, 1, 40, 119, 148, 149, 161, 166
routines, 12, 116. *See also* rituals

S

safety, psychological, 139. *See also* trust
SAP SE, 76
savings from remote work, 62–63. *See also* reinvesting in employees
scheduling, 152–153. *See also* meetings; time differences
schools, 79
screen logging, 37. *See also* monitoring of employees
self-awareness, 119
self-care, 75, 85, 173. *See also* mental health
self-esteem, 79
self-reflection, 117
separation, physical, 5
side projects, 40, 119, 121, 163, 166

signing off, 83, 88, 117–118
Silen pods, 106
Silicon Valley, 160
skills, 65–66, 67. *See also* communication; training
skills, hard, 133–135, 176
skills, soft, 130–133, 176
Slack, 36, 42, 49, 52, 53, 56
small talk, 24
SocGen (Société Générale), 124
social dynamics, 14. *See also* interactions
social interaction. *See* interactions; isolation
social media, 36, 143
socializing, 63–64, 156. *See also* interactions; office culture
    mental health and, 88
    remote work and, 20–21
    workplaces designed for, 154
Société Générale (SocGen), 124
spaces, informal, 57
spontaneity, communication and, 55
Spotify, 105
stakeholders, communication with, 138
stand-up meetings, 57, 94, 102–103
startups, 137–138
status updates, 93–94, 103
stress, 34–35, 77, 107. *See also* mental health
structure, 12–13, 14, 116. *See also* rituals
subscriptions, 70
support, 82–83

T

tables, 109–110. *See also* home office
Takako's Methods
    consolidation of places, 23–25
    focus, 119–121
    meetings, 102–104
    mental health, 86–88
    reinvestment in employees, 68–71
    streamlining communication, 55–57
    trust, 42–43
talent. *See* team members; workers
tasks, prioritizing, 116–117
team members. *See also* workers
    communication between, 132, 163
    focus of, 118–121
    trust and, 31
Teams, 49, 102
technology, 171–172. *See also* communication; home office
    collaborative tools, 52, 53
    comfort with, 168
    learning about, 167
    providing, 65
    reliance on, 5
    rituals and, 18

training on, 51. *see also* training
trust and, 35
Zoom, 53, 90, 91, 97, 99, 102. *see also* meetings
thinking, divergent, 104
time, 177
ownership of, 146. *see also* freedom
savings in, 63
time blocking, 112, 116, 117, 175
time differences, 51, 96, 97, 134, 172
Time Insight, 41–42
to-do lists, 116–117
tracking software, 37. *See also* monitoring of employees
training, 51, 65–66, 67, 68–69, 145, 172. *See also* skills
transitions, 20. *See also* place; rituals
transparency, 40, 41
travel, 62, 161. *See also* commute
Trello, 50
trust, 28–43, 79, 137, 170–171. *See also* privacy; relationships
barriers to, 32–35
building, 33, 85
burnout and, 34–35
communication and, 30, 31, 32–35, 39
components of, 29–30
culture and, 33–34
importance of, 30
investing in employees and, 64
monitoring and, 35–38, 42–43
organizational, 31–32
solving issues of, 38–42
between team members, 31
technology and, 35
Twitter, 143

U

UBS, 125
Up in the Air, 161
upskilling, 65–66, 67, 68–69, 145, 172

V

vaccines, 2
Verdant Management, 89–90
videoconferencing, 89, 91. *See also* meetings; technology; Zoom
Virtual Commute, 20
voice calls, advantages of, 95–96
VoxEU, 19

W

Wally Health, 135
Washington Post, 141
Washingtonian, 141–143
Wikipedia, 46
women, 165. *See also* mothers
work, asynchronous, 46, 60
work, changes in, 2–3
work, remote. *See* remote work
work boundaries, 117, 120
work culture, in Japan, 6
work for other companies, 40, 119, 121, 163, 166
work from home. *See* home office; remote work
workdays
mental health and, 81–82
non-linear, 60
workers. *See also* team members
attracting, 67, 124–125, 148, 150
diversity/inclusion and, 165–166
new hires, 63
new type of, 144–147, 176. *see also* Gen Z; Millennials; office, hybrid
personality types, 163–164
power of, 143–144, 147
reinvesting in, 64–71, 172–173. *see also* training
reluctance to return to physical office, 142–143, 146, 176
unsuited to remote work, 164–165
view of remote work, 125
work outside company, 40, 119, 121, 163, 166
work-from-home fund, 70–71. *See also* home office
work-life balance, 74, 82, 83, 88, 146. *See also* mental health
workplace. *See* home office; office, hybrid; office, physical; place; remote work
workshops, online, 103–104
Workspace, 41–42
World Health Organization, 77

Z

zero mind, 113
Zoom, 53, 90, 91, 97, 99, 102. *See also* meetings
Zuckerberg, Mark, 160

ABOUT THE AUTHOR

Photo by Naonori Takada

TAKAKO HIRATA works at the frontier of healthcare and technology. She is Head of International Business Development at Rohto Pharmaceutical, where she oversees five subsidiary CEOs and leads more than one hundred remote teammates across five continents. She is also a Board Member of Mentholatum. She has also built an online technology-focused media hub called InTech.Media, which seeks to bridge the information gap between Japan and the United States. Previously she was at Procter & Gamble, where she oversaw major product lines such as Febreze, before becoming a Marketing Design Manager and leading branding strategist in P&G's US and China markets. She later took on the role of Director of Brand Strategy at Aeon. Currently, she is an Executive MBA candidate at UCLA-NUS and the only Japanese certificate holder of the 2020 MIT-Harvard

Medical School Healthcare Innovation Bootcamp. She lives in Tokyo, Japan, but she leads from everywhere.

You can visit her personal website at https://takakohirata.com/en/

You can visit her media website at https://intech.media/en/